THE SEVEN KEYS TO MANAGING STRATEGIC ACCOUNTS

SALLIE SHERMAN
JOSEPH SPERRY
SAM REESE

McGraw-Hill
New York Chicago San Francisco Lisbon
London Madrid Mexico City Milan
Montreal New Delhi San Juan
Seoul Singapore Sydney Toronto

1 2 3 4 5 6 7 8 9 0 DOC /DOC 0 9 8 7 6 5 4 3

ISBN 0-07-141752-4

McGraw-Hill books are available at special quantity discounts to use as premiums and sales promotions, or for use in corporate training programs. For more information, please write to the Director of Special Sales, McGraw-Hill, Professional Publishing, 2 Penn Plaza, New York, NY 10121-2298. Or contact your local bookstore.

This publication is designed to provide accurate and authoritative information in regard to the subject matter covered. It is sold with the understanding that neither the authors nor the publisher are engaged in rendering legal, accounting, or other professional service. If legal advice or other expert assistance is required, the services of a competent professional should be sought.

—From a Declaration of Principles jointly adopted by a Committee of the American Bar Association and a Committee of Publishers.

This book is printed on recycled, acid-free paper containing a minimum of 50% recycled de-inked fiber.

Library of Congress Cataloging-in-Publication Data
Sherman, Sallie.
    The seven keys to managing strategic accounts / by Sallie Sherman, Joseph Sperry, and Sam Reese.
        p. cm.
Includes bibliographical references.
    ISBN 0-07-141752-4 (hardcover : alk. paper)
    1. Selling—Key accounts. 2. Marketing—Key accounts 3. Strategic planning.   I. Sperry, Joseph. II. Reese, Sam (Samuel J.) III. Title.
    HF5438.8.K48S54 2003
    658.15'11—dc21
                                        2002156091

To our families, friends, and customers who have nurtured and supported us throughout this process.

CONTENTS

PART 3

FROM ANALYSIS TO ACTION . . . TICONDEROGA
CHEMICAL AND STRATEGIC ACCOUNT
MANAGEMENT: THE PAYOFF

Chapter 9

Conclusion: From Analysis to Action:
Moving the Game Forward   173

WHY THIS BOOK?

This book grew out of two questions our clients most often ask when they are managing strategic accounts: "What are the challenges others have faced with strategic accounts, and how can we overcome them?"

During our years of experience, through constantly changing business conditions, we have tested, retested, and revised many of our original answers to these questions. One of our enduring insights remains: There is no by-the-numbers approach to implementing strategic account management. Every firm must come at it a little differently. At the same time, though, this book lists the strategic account management challenges our clients have most often struggled with. We also present proven ways to overcome those challenges.

Our clients and colleagues encouraged us to consider how our experience might benefit a wider audience. This book is our response, crystallizing what we have learned in strategic account management. Our goal is to help you save time and money as you implement or refine a strategic account management program.

WHAT QUALIFIES US TO ADDRESS THIS TOPIC?

This book is a joint effort from S4 Consulting, Inc. and Miller Heiman, Inc.

S4 Consulting, a leading-edge relationship management firm, has helped business-to-business clients use strategic account management to improve their business performance since 1986. S4 Consulting uniquely focuses on gaining the internal firmwide commitment and support that are so critical for the success of strategic account management. Huge benefits occur when sales and other departments work together more effectively, when interdepartmental barriers are lowered, and when everyone is headed in roughly the same direction.

Information S4 Consulting personnel have gathered and processed from interviews with thousands of strategic account contacts helps us better guide companies to optimize those relationships. This outside-in approach can pay huge dividends. S4 Consulting's commitment to using strategic account management to improve business performance, has led us to design, conduct, and co-sponsor SAMA's annual Strategic Account Management Performance Award for the USA. Many of the case studies in this book are from nominees and recipients of that award.

Miller Heiman, a leading developer and provider of sales development solutions for sales organizations and professionals around the world since 1978, has made building exceptional sales organizations its single-most important accomplishment. The Miller Heiman team of consultants has helped more than one million sales professionals use the right strategies and tactics to win business and turn prospects into customers for life. Miller Heiman has pioneered several highly respected sales process programs, including *Strategic Selling®*, *Conceptual Selling®*, *Large Account Management Process*[sm], and *Negotiate Success*[sm].

Both firms are committed to helping companies improve their bottom-line performance by effectively managing their customer assets. A book focused on strategic account management seemed a natural topic for collaboration.

Because people seem to learn best from comparing what works with what doesn't, each chapter includes examples of both. The firms cited as positive examples have verified the facts describing their cases. We have disguised the negative examples by creating composite cases: for each example of what doesn't work, there are 5 to 10 more cases with similar situations.

WHO WILL BENEFIT FROM READING THIS BOOK?

There are a number of readers for this book. Our primary audience is any decision maker whose primary task is optimizing the firm's assets and anyone who wants to manage—as assets—that small percentage of customers who usually provide a disproportionate share of the firm's revenue/profits. These readers may be starting or refining an existing strategic account management program. The cases and insights should be an invaluable resource for any executive, drawn to developing systematic sales and management processes, who wishes to avoid critical and costly errors in doing so. Early in the book we contend that unless these executives—CEOs, COOs, VPs of Finance, and decision makers from all functional areas—are aligned to support the strategic account management program's goals and objectives, the program will almost certainly tailspin in costly flames.

> **Our primary audience is any decision maker whose primary task is optimizing the firm's assets . . .**

Other readers who can benefit from this book are the very best of those who manage strategic account relationships—a complex, challenging, and often very rewarding task. People who do this job well are relationship assets in their own right. We have found their commitment to self-development very high indeed. They are always looking for ways to improve their skills and their overall management approach, to improve service and relationship quality to their assigned customers.

WHAT IS A STRATEGIC ACCOUNT?

Strategic accounts are those customers who most readily help a firm achieve its strategic and financial goals.

They are chosen as strategic accounts because they have met specific criteria and they are most likely to provide a return on the higher level of investment that managing such accounts requires. These customers may be large, they may be small (targeted emerging accounts, for example), but they have strategic significance for the supplier.

Strategic accounts are those customers that most readily help a firm achieve its strategic and financial goals.

This book will use three words interchangeably to describe such customers: strategic account, account, and customer. Although all customers are important, there are certain customers you cannot afford to ignore or live without. You must treat strategic accounts differently (unless they request otherwise) and invest more in them. You need to select and invest in these accounts wisely.

S4 CONSULTING ACKNOWLEDGMENTS

This book is the product of years of collaboration.

First, Joe and I would especially like to acknowledge Dan Shaffer, our partner and friend at S4 Consulting for 20 years. His wisdom and systematic problem solving have provided inestimable value to us, our company, and our clients.

Second, we would like to thank some of our colleagues, particularly Doug Bosse, Dave Jones, Steve Vucelich, Len Shaffer, Jose Acevedo, and Nicholas Wolfson, who have contributed significantly to our conceptual and methodological development. We would also like to acknowledge Jim Guilkey, Sally Trethewey, Rosa Yeh, Maribeth Quinn, Wes Mayer, Karin Huey, Urko Wood, Suzanne Lowe, Sharon Bierman, Mike Sternad, Sarah Volker, Barbara Gossman, and Erin Hinkle, who have provided valuable support. Together we have learned to make a difference.

Third, we thank our business partners, those from whom we gained new ways to look at business, service quality, and meeting client needs: Valarie Zeithaml, Bob Wayland, Bob Archibald, Kaj Storbacka, CRM Finland, and Lisa Napolitano, Director of The Strategic Account Management Association. Each helped guide our thinking in managing relationship assets.

Finally we thank those at Miller Heiman with whom we have worked so closely: Sam Reese, Jason Buma, Jenna Poinier, Harry Magure, Ryan Olsen, and Erin Anderson. Without their efforts and feedback, this would have been a very different book.

MILLER HEIMAN INC. ACKNOWLEDGMENTS

We would like to express our appreciation to Joe Sperry and Sallie Sherman of S4 Consulting. Their knowledge and past experiences greatly contributed to the concepts and methodology that made this book possible. We would also like to extend our appreciation to Damon Jones, Jason Buma, and Jenna Poinier for their careful editing and skillful review of the material. We are also grateful to Harry Magure for providing his legal expertise throughout this process, Ryan Olsen for his project management efforts that went into the completion of the project, and Erin Anderson for his graphic design contributions. Lastly, we would like to thank Catherine Dassopoulos of McGraw-Hill for facilitating a smooth and enjoyable publishing experience.

FOR THE READER THINKING, "I CAN'T READ THE WHOLE BOOK. WHICH CHAPTERS WOULD HELP ME MOST?"

We suggest starting with the Introduction, which provides our approach and general thesis. After that, here is a listing, with abstracts, of the book's eight remaining chapters. The abstracts will help readers get right to the issues that concern them most.

Introduction: What Is Strategic Account Management?

The Introduction defines strategic account management and contains a high-level look at its particular rewards and challenges.

Part 1: Getting Everyone Headed in Roughly the Same Direction

Key 1: Define strategic account management as a business rather than a sales initiative. If a firm tries to implement strategic account management purely as a sales initiative, chances are good that only sales will "own" the account. This means that the sales team will have to spend at least half its time internally marketing to functions that may feel no special urgency to meet the needs of strategic accounts. Cross-functional executives need to align the entire organization—from other executives down—in owning the strategic account relationships. In our experience, that is the fastest way to optimal performance in strategic account programs.

Key 2: Create firm alignment and commitment to meet strategic accounts' needs and expectations. Everyone in the organization needs to understand why strategic accounts are so critical and how they can best serve those customers. Strategic account management can fail when one or two departments remain embedded in the status quo. Unless all departments and all employees are committed to supporting the strategic accounts' needs and expectations, account management will always be one customer phone call away from disappointment. Lacking commitment, the firm will find it very difficult to gain the momentum needed to shift from an internal focus to a business strategy.

Key 3: Start with the right number of the right strategic accounts. Firms are sometimes tempted to start big—by simply declaring their 65 largest revenue producers "strategic accounts" (whether or not they are profitable). If a supplier starts with its 65 largest customers, aggressively promoting the customer management program's improved service levels, it will very likely find broken processes and systems early in the journey. These may require months to fix and, while they are being fixed, customers are not receiving their promised service levels. Starting with too many customers makes it difficult for the program to demonstrate success and leverage its initial investments. Starting with the wrong customers is almost as bad. If a supplier doesn't do some sort of portfolio analysis of potential strategic accounts, it can find itself making large investments for little or no return.

Part 2: Tactical Issues in Strategic Account Management

Key 4: Create human resources support for strategic account managers. Questions firms need to answer while developing a customer management program include: (1) How do we find account managers? (2) How do we develop account managers? (3) How do we assign account managers? and (4) How do we pay account managers?

Key 5: Create firmwide relationships at multiple levels of relationships between the firm and its most critical accounts. We have often seen account managers developing and maintaining strong relationships with the tactical customer employees such as technicians or purchasing people. While it is important to develop such relationships, the account manager has additional tasks: (1) developing deep and multilevel relationships within the account—from executives down; (2) determining the strategic account's various buyer influences; and (3) identifying, within their own firms, those who could best help manage relationships within the strategic account. The goal here is to establish a firmwide relationship, based on ongoing parallel linkages between supplier and customer.

Key 6: Regularly quantify and communicate the value received from and delivered to strategic accounts. To succeed, strategic account management requires solid returns on its investments. The program's executive sponsors and those serving the account, perhaps working with the finance people, should determine the customer's long-term relationship asset value and its replacement cost. They should also be able to quantify the value delivered to customers. Without continually quantifying and communicating value, there is no way to justify relationship investments internally or to justify a premium price externally.

Key 7: Use technology judiciously. There is a difference between being technology-driven and technology-supported. The technology-driven company, occasionally without determining its overall needs, invests in the "latest and greatest" technological breakthrough. The technology-supported company determines what it needs and then finds the best tools to support its strategic ends. We have seen that a technology-driven approach to strategic accounts can be a very expensive bandwagon to hop on. Technological caution can save a firm millions of dollars.

Part 3: Conclusion

Conclusion: From Analysis to Action. This chapter will review the keys and benefits of strategic account management, provide a high-level implementation roadmap, and offer some next steps.

For additional information about us, please contact:

S4 Consulting

1480 Manning Parkway	1595 Meadow Wood Lane, Suite 2
Powell, Ohio 43065	Reno, Nevada 89502
614-786-7300	877-678-0269
www.s4consulting.com	www.millerheiman.com

Introduction: What Is Strategic Account Management?

Let's begin by considering:

1. What is strategic account management?
2. How does strategic account management differ from key account selling?
3. What are the benefits of strategic account management?
4. What are the challenges of strategic account management?

WHAT IS STRATEGIC ACCOUNT MANAGEMENT?

Strategic account management is a systematic process for managing key interactions and relationships with critical accounts. Writers sometimes quote the Pareto Principle to describe strategic accounts: 20 percent of the customers generate 80 percent of the revenue/profit. It's usually an apt comparison, although the numbers can vary dramatically if the firm's strategy has targeted emerging or medium-sized accounts. Still, strategic accounts tend to provide a disproportionate share of a firm's revenue/profit. We call such customers co-destiny accounts.

The supplier's future tends to be intertwined with these accounts' success. With clients whose contribution is that critical, strategic account management can play a crucial role in a firm's marketing strategy. That's why successful strategic account management tends to be a firmwide initiative, systematically and proactively delivering strategic solutions to multiple contacts at targeted accounts—to capture a dominant share over time.

Strategic account managers are salespersons who must generate profitable revenue, quarter-to-quarter and over the long term. At the same time, they are general managers, overseeing assigned relationships as separate assets in the customer portfolio. Businesspeople sometimes distinguish between salespeople who are hunters and those who are gatherers—those who get the business and those who manage the business afterwards. True strategic account managers (SAMs) are both and neither of these classifications: they are hunters but within their assigned accounts, continually working to increase account share. They also must manage those account relationships, and be accountable for ongoing and long-term financial growth.

> **Strategic accounts tend to provide a disproportionate share of a firm's revenue/profit. We call them co-destiny accounts.**

HOW DOES STRATEGIC ACCOUNT MANAGEMENT DIFFER FROM KEY ACCOUNT SELLING?

Most of the time, the sales team initiates strategic account programs. Sales may see an opportunity to generate more revenue by focusing its efforts on the larger accounts. Sales often begins these initiatives with what we call a key account selling approach. Key account selling is a part of strategic account management but it is not the same thing. The distinction between the two is important for our discussion. The following chart distinguishes between these two (of many) approaches in managing an important account. Figure 1-1 isolates the behaviors of a key account selling approach and a strategic account management program. The chart concentrates on behaviors because of the ever-present problem of program names: a supplier may have a key account selling program called a strategic account management program (common) or a strategic account management program called a key account selling program (also common). Our primary interest is in what these firms *do* with their crucial customers.

Successful strategic account management tends to be a firmwide initiative, systematically and proactively delivering strategic solutions to multiple contacts at targeted accounts— to capture a dominant share over time.

KEY ACCOUNT SELLING PROGRAMS AND STRATEGIC ACCOUNT MANAGEMENT PROGRAMS: A COMPARISON[1]

Key account selling approaches tend to be initiated by sales, they tend to work on a shorter planning horizon, to measure success primarily on incremental, perhaps quarter-to-quarter, revenue, and they tend to sell mostly existing products to a small number of people within a large number of accounts.

In many cases, these programs require a great deal of internal selling because sales, while usually not customizing offerings, may come up with creative discount, financing, delivery, or service options. Their creativity puts pressure on other departments to do things differently for large customers. This

---

[1]   © S4 Consulting, Inc.

F I G U R E   1 – 1

Key Account Selling Programs and Strategic Account Management Programs: A Comparison

Key Account Selling Programs		Strategic Account Management Programs

1. Under a year
2. By revenue potential
3. Vertical market
	Planning Horizon Customer Segmentation	1. 1 to 3 years
		2. By revenue potential and strategic criteria:
		  a. How they prefer to buy
		  b. Willingness to partner
		  c. Complementary competencies

4. Existing products 5. Some custom solutions	**Offerings**	3. Existing products 4. Custom solutions 5. Firm competencies
6. Products and service	**Differentiates by**	6. Value delivered over time
7. Account manager 8. Sales team	**Primary Account Responsibility**	7. Account manager who can commit resources 8. Cross-functional team 9. Supplier executives
9. Short- and long-term revenue 10. Share of customer 11. Competitors	**Primary Concerns**	10. Profitability 11. Short- and long-term revenue and profitability 12. Account's business challenges 13. Share of customer
12. 10–25	**Number of Accounts per Manager**	14. 1–5
13. Half salary, half commission 14. Sales/product plans	**Account Manager Compensation**	15. Generous salary with some incentive bonus 16. Overall account plan 17. P&L of account relationship
15. Sales 16. Vertical expertise 17. Understands customer's business	**Account Manager Skills Required**	18. Sales and/or general management skills 19. Strategic thinking 20. Excels in ability to influence without authority 21. Deep understanding of customer's and supplier's business

pressure can leave those other functional departments seeing key accounts as key irritations.

We know a manufacturer whose sales group decided to develop a key account selling approach. The firm kicked off the program by announcing to its 15 largest customers how great the new effort would be, and started coming up with innovative ways to serve those customers. But after they made creative commitments to the customers, internal functions continually blocked their way. Those departments saw no particular reason to do things differently. Sales spent so much time marketing internally that one sales representative joked that he needed to carry cushions around for his knees because he was begging so much. The results were not as humorous when the supplier's responsiveness and reliability—as well as account satisfaction numbers—declined markedly. At the end of the year, the key accounts program was serving only a few of the original customers— and those were not being served very effectively.

Key account selling approaches tend to work on a shorter planning horizon, to measure success primarily on incremental, perhaps quarter-to-quarter, revenue, and tend to sell mostly existing products . . . within a large number of accounts.

When the manufacturer tried to determine how to improve the situation, those in manufacturing said, "You have to understand: sales' dream deal is our worst nightmare." They said that when the sales teams promise a dramatically reduced delivery time for a small custom order, that lowers the entire manufacturing operation's line utilization and slows other critical production runs (both of which were major components in manufacturing's compensation). The sales team must realize that departments may have solid reasons for resisting a sales mandate—even if the initiative proposed would generate

significant short-term revenue. If the program is going to succeed, the entire organization must understand and align
around the account selling program's goals—particularly if the
firm ultimately wants to move to a true strategic account management process. It is, at best, an uphill battle for sales to develop a strategic account management program by itself.

What Are the Benefits of Strategic Account Management?

The benefits from a strong strategic account management program can be huge. At its best, strategic account management
can offer a competitive advantage, the key to greater loyalty,
and the road to higher profitability.

Strategic account management can offer a competitive advantage, the key to greater loyalty, and the road to higher profitability.

One of the more dramatic examples of what strategic account
management programs can
achieve financially comes from
Boise Office Solutions. Until 1992,
Boise Office Solutions (BOS) was a
dual distributor with one channel
selling directly to business and a
wholesale channel selling to office
products dealers. This dual-distri-
bution business model deepened
channel conflicts during a time
when BOS's largest customers
were becoming much more sophisticated—and much more demanding. In 1992, BOS reinvented its business model by selling
its wholesale-distribution business and establishing a national
account management program. The incremental revenue generated by the BOS national account program—even allowing
for revenue growth by acquisition—is dramatic:

    1992: $52,000,000
    1994: $250,000,000
    1996: $550,000,000
    1998: $1,000,000,000

2000: $1,500,000,000

2001: $1,600,000,000

We will hear more about Boise Office Solutions later in the book and provide other successes of customer management, such as Honeywell Automation and Control Solutions, which serves a dozen of the world's largest oil companies. In two years it grew business 61 percent in a flat-to-declining market and cut selling costs 40 percent, while moving to a systematic account management program. We will also see how Reynolds & Reynolds' Enterprise Solutions Group generated a 55 percent compounded growth rate on sales to its largest single customer, Southeast Toyota.

The payoffs from an effective strategic account management program can be significant—and they are usually much more than dollars. A well-designed and well-executed strategic account management program can minimize, or in some cases, eliminate competition. The more quickly you get that program up and running, the more quickly you can realize those payoffs. This book will guide readers through the implementation pitfalls and to those payoffs.

What Are the Challenges of Implementing Strategic Account Management?

We have asked directors of successful account management programs what it took to create that success. Few directors have said, "Piece of cake. We got it right the first time." At the same time, these directors tend to agree that they received tremendous personal and professional benefits from systematically managing critical customer relationships: the approach has usually made account relationships significantly more fulfilling

Even the most successful directors emphasize the challenges at the beginning and stress how much less costly it is to do it right the first time.

and more profitable than the more typical transactional relationships. After success and clear returns, it's much easier to
support strategic account management. But even the most successful directors emphasize the challenges at the beginning and
stress how much less costly it is to do it right the first time.

Strategic account management programs falter when firms
underestimate the time, resource requirements, and complexity
of rolling out the program. We have worked with very successful business leaders who started out believing they could dele-
gate the entire implementation of the program to a middle manager and completely roll it out in three to six months of that
manager's free time. These firms are very profitable and run by
very intelligent businesspeople. But having never implemented
strategic account manage-
ment—and lacking any real-world
guidebooks on the subject—it's not
that surprising when their strategic
account initiatives do not succeed
the first time. Decision makers un-
derstandably rely on what they
know, which may be sales or operational models. These models are
unfortunately inappropriate for
implementing strategic account
management. They tend to create
unintended consequences in im-
plementation—as we'll see throughout this book. It's much like
playing ice hockey with a tennis racket. You may work very
hard, but the chances are low that you will score, and you will almost certainly get beaten up some. This book provides appropriate models, thereby limiting the number of your implementation
bruises—and wasted resources.

Creating a systematic way to manage strategic accounts is a little like putting down the road as you're driving on it . . .

Creating a systematic way to manage strategic accounts is
a little like putting down the road as you're driving on it: You
must maintain your firm's financial performance while reinventing the way it serves its most critical customers. That is perhaps the greatest challenge in implementing strategic account
management.

Thanks to the experience of cartoon character Dilbert and others, most workers are now highly suspicious of new organizational change initiatives. This means that strategic account management—or almost any major change initiative—fails if it is perceived as a program *du jour*. Employees have seen far too many programs started and then stopped. One secret of successful strategic account management programs is that they start small, as a critical part of the business strategy, and then migrate to become standard operating procedure as soon as they have demonstrated their success.

Reinventing the way you serve critical customers usually requires an organizational shift from internal efficiencies to external effectiveness. This shift is particularly challenging because in many companies, most employees have inward-focused performance measures and, on average, only 30 to 40 percent of employees ever interact with customers. To achieve this kind of shift, the entire firm needs to understand viscerally how critical these strategic customers are, and start to own them. Here is a communication, educational, and performance opportunity worth the challenge.

Unless the supplier removes its internal cross-functional barriers, the strategic account—and the strategic account manager—will be forced to try to jump over them.

For the shift to take root, you must include all relevant departments in the planning, goal setting, and process redesign for account management. Having their say will make it easier to lower any walls that may have risen between them. Unless the supplier removes its internal cross-functional barriers, the strategic account—and the strategic account manager—will be forced to try to jump over them.

The most sophisticated account management programs we know live in organizations committed to co-creating value for customers whose destiny is intertwined with their own.

That's simply a way of life for firms such as Marriott International, Boise Office Solutions, and IBM, all of which earned cases in this book.

The game of business has changed dramatically in the last decade. Ten years ago, companies could often function more as a golf team—a group of talented individuals, each bent on winning his own way. That approach won't work very well in the global economy, rife with consolidation, mergers, and wildly varied expectations. Many companies instead must respond to markets and customers more like a basketball or hockey team, with everyone working together to win the game. To extend the metaphor: in straight golf, there are no assists. The new business model, however, is all about continuing assists: working together more effectively.

The new business model is all about continuing assists: working together more effectively.

To respond as rapidly as market and customer conditions change usually requires much greater interdependence—both within the organization and between the firm and its strategic accounts. Firms usually should align around and work toward the goals and strategies driving customer management. Firms that can reinvent their business models while maintaining financial performance, firms that can remove departmental barriers and gain commitments from all functions to play the same customer-centered game, tend to enjoy the rewards of long-term financial success. As one example, let us turn to the Reynolds & Reynolds—Southeast Toyota story to see the value a strategic alliance can create.

REYNOLDS & REYNOLDS—SOUTHEAST TOYOTA: AN EXAMPLE OF ALIGNMENT

Reynolds & Reynolds is a $1 billion company headquartered in Dayton, Ohio, which provides integrated information-management solutions to the automotive retail marketplace. Its products include retail and enterprise-management systems, networking, e-business applications, web services, CRM, consulting, and leasing services. The Enterprise Solutions Group at Reynolds manages strategic accounts. Enterprise Solutions has 15 partnership executives, and they work with the 20 largest automotive retail and distributor groups in North America, helping them achieve outstanding business results. Enterprise Solutions accounts generate more than $90 million in annual revenue.

The account in this case is Southeast Toyota Distributors (SET) based in Deerfield Beach, Florida. It is one of the most respected automotive companies in the world, with exclusive distribution rights to market new Toyotas in the southeastern United States. SET has 163 dealer locations that outperform all others in the industry, regardless of brand, in nearly every measurable category—sales per outlet, profit per outlet, dealer satisfaction, and customer satisfaction. SET also owns two other companies that offer financial services, such as insurance and extended warranties, to more than 1,500 retailers. SET and its affiliated companies have annual sales of $7 billion.

In 1997, Reynolds' Enterprise Solutions Group started working with SET, helping it achieve its business objectives. Gary Coveyou, the Reynolds' SET Account Manager, created a dedicated account team for SET with Reynolds employees from the following areas:

- Sales and Marketing
- Service and Support
- Consulting Services
- Automark Web Services
- Project Management and Development
- Financial Services
- Document Solutions
- Reynolds CRM Services
- Reynolds Software Solutions

At Reynolds & Reynolds, strategic account management is not simply a sales initiative. It is clearly a business initiative. With this team, Coveyou developed an account playbook for

SET that laid out how Reynolds needed to sell, deliver, and support its business solutions. The SET account team realized from the start that it is just as important to build solid relationships as it is to deliver great technical solutions.

The SET account team realized from the start that it is just as important to build solid relationships as it is to deliver great technical solutions.

Reynolds had started the relationship before 1997 by selling to individual SET dealerships its dealer management system, an enterprise resource planning (ERP) system for automotive dealers with accounting, inventory, vehicle management, CRM, and other functions. In 1997, Coveyou and his account team sold SET corporate on the benefits of working with Reynolds & Reynolds to develop the next generation of its dealer management system. Because it was a critical step in its long-range strategy, Southeast Toyota dealers then bought the current Reynolds & Reynolds dealer management systems. Both firms realized that such an alliance would lead to greater business results for many years. Coveyou had seen that Southeast Toyota was the perfect partner—and a marquee account—for such joint development.

By 1999, Reynolds had installed its current dealer management systems in 80 percent of SET dealerships. While installing these systems, Reynolds people were also interviewing more than 200 SET associates to capture their requirements and develop the functional specifications for Reynolds' next generation of solutions and services.

THE BENEFITS TO SOUTHEAST TOYOTA

When we asked Reynolds & Reynolds to quantify the benefits both they and Southeast Toyota had received from the alliance, their relationship was such that representatives from both firms sat down together to determine that dual value. There were several major areas of value-added for Southeast Toyota:

- Eighty percent of Southeast Toyota dealerships are using Reynolds Dealer Management systems. Reynolds has discovered that those dealers are, on average, realizing $200,000 more in annual net profits than SET dealers not using the system. This is substantial considering dealers are categorically small businesses.

- Since SET began using Reynolds' web services, it has seen a 52 percent increase in generated leads. The percentage of these leads that closed is up a whopping 45 percent from last year—more than 6,500 new vehicles sold. It's hard to come up with an average price for a Toyota, given price ranges between $20,000 for a Corolla to more than $55,000 for a Land Cruiser. If we use a conservative estimate of $22,000 per vehicle, though, Reynolds' Internet lead-generation system brought SET more than $143 million in incremental revenue last year.

Reynolds' Internet lead-generation system brought SET more than $143 million in incremental revenue last year.

- SET also realized significant savings in its parts department. As Wayne Crater, SET's Director of Parts Operations, says, "The partnership between SET and Reynolds & Reynolds has paid significant benefits to both our dealers and SET. Dealer parts departments have experienced increased sales, due in part to the advanced marketing tools from R&R, while at the same time [dealers] have lowered their inventory values and decreased levels of obsolete inventory. In addition, the ability of R&R to provide SET parts managers with several software enhancements minimized the new system learning curve and [gave them] a system tailored to their requirements. All . . . these accomplishments translate into increased profitability for both our dealers and SET."

- Key Improvements for SET Parts Operations . . .

  1. Parts and Accessory sales have grown in excess of 21 percent, or $475 million, during the past five years to more than $2.26 billion. Reynolds has provided an inventory-control parts marketing system, which enabled SET to reach this growth, increase their profits, and achieve operational efficiencies.
  2. Of the 163 dealers, 114 were stocking excessive obsolescence inventory. Reynolds helped to reduce the count by 65 locations, from 114 dealers to 49.

THE BENEFITS TO REYNOLDS & REYNOLDS

- Since the partnership began in 1997, Reynolds' sales to SET have jumped from $1.8 million to more than $16 million in 2001.
- Reynolds' sales' five-year compound annual growth rate with SET is 55 percent per year.
- Over the last five years, Reynolds' document solutions sales to SET have leaped more than 500 percent, its services revenue from SET has increased more than 500 percent, and Reynolds was selected as SET's exclusive provider of web services.

The more value Reynolds delivers, the more value Southeast Toyota provides. It is a classic example of what is possible with strategic account management.

THE FUTURE OF THE REYNOLDS & REYNOLDS SET RELATIONSHIP

Reynolds & Reynolds is hardly resting on its laurels in the SET relationship. Gary Coveyou is currently implementing a plan to provide financing and support services to all SET dealers for Toyota's Technical Information System. This is the first time Reynolds has ever financed and supported a third-party system. But Reynolds' goal continues to be helping SET meet its business objectives, and SET is a solid reference for new Reynolds' prospects—a powerful marketing aid in a fiercely competitive marketplace.

Rick Boyer, Reynolds & Reynolds' vice president, Enterprise Solutions Group, sums up his feelings about the firm's strategic account management: "The foundation for Reynolds & Reynolds' enterprise account management model is a combination of account strategy, account planning, a dedicated account team of highly skilled employees, and a careful integration of the customer into this process to ensure we deliver a complete set of value-based solutions. . . . Our model has resulted in significant success for both our customers and for Reynolds."

A word about strategic account management in a bear market: Some readers might argue that the best time to implement strategic account management is in a bull market. We are not ignoring the economy—we can see those parentheses on our 401K's as well as anyone. But we believe this book's keys are even more valid in a bear market because strategic accounts remain a supplier's greatest assets. In the *Harvard Management Update*, David Stouffer quotes Adrian Slywotsky as saying, "In uncertain times, your best customers provide an even greater share of the profits. It's important, especially now, to see the world through their eyes."[2] Our experience has been that, even in good times, many suppliers tend

> **Even in good times, many suppliers tend to underinvest in the customer relationships on whose future they depend.**

---

[2] Stauffer, David (2002). "Five Missteps to Avoid in Volatile Times," (p. 3) from *Harvard Management Update*, September, Volume 7, Number 9

to underinvest in the customer relationships on whose future they depend.

That would be especially unwise at a time when accounts are hungry for value in any form. Each of our seven keys applies to protecting as well as expanding strategic accounts.

Getting Everyone Headed in Roughly the Same Direction: What Didn't Work

Orson B. Counter was the accounts receivables manager at Federated Tire. His professional life was governed by two rules: (1) Federated's customers must pay within 30 days and (2) if they did not pay, he gave them one warning before he cut them off past 60 days. If Orson broke either of these rules, his boss, Ed Bolton, Federated's comptroller, came down on him hard—"for his own good," as he often told Orson. Ed, whose leadership style had been compared to that of Benito Mussolini, had done so much for Orson's own good that Orson was terrified of him and kept past-due receivables nonexistent. Ed saw this fear and the absence of past-due accounts as triumphs of progressive management.

Federated Tire's largest customer (30 percent of gross sales) was Dutton Retail, a national account that was having major problems with the recession, which created severe cash-flow problems and forced it to stretch out payments to suppliers. Because Federated's marketing/sales department was killing itself trying to maintain Dutton's order levels, it never occurred to marketing/sales to emphasize to other functional departments how critical Dutton was to Federated. Marketing/sales assumed that everyone *had* to know Dutton was Federated's number-one customer.

Everyone didn't know. Orson knew that Dutton's revenue levels were higher than most, but his performance evaluations were not based on knowing strategic accounts. He was evaluated on those two rules, and as Dutton stretched out the payments even farther, it broke Ed Bolton's first rule . . . it went beyond 30 days. On day #31, Orson sent out the dunning letter that Ed had written, a masterpiece (thought Ed) at declaring that customers were *not* going to take advantage of Federated.

John Reardon, Dutton's accounts payable manager, was neither particularly guilty nor motivated by any wish to take advantage of Federated. But he did feel anger pure enough to cut through steel. He knew that Dutton's marketing managers were working with Federated and couldn't understand the motivation of the individual who had sent him and his company such a letter. He filed and forgot it.

Time passed. At 60 days, Dutton had still not paid the bill and Orson sent Dutton a letter that went far beyond dunning. It first cut off all product deliveries. It then mentioned—none too subtly—the massive law firm held on retainer.

If Reardon had been angry after receiving the first letter, he was furious at the second. He took it in trembling hands to his CEO, Stan Dutton, who read it and then reread it, his face growing more purple. Dutton picked up the phone and called Federated's CEO and, in an icy tone, told him that he was overnighting a check for the entire amount owed and that—by the way—Dutton would *never* buy tires from Federated again.

This story is true, with the names changed to protect the guilty. We've been surprised at how many businesspeople have said the same thing had happened at their firm. Chapters 1, 2, and 3 focus on how to get your departments heading in roughly the same direction—toward meeting the needs of strategic accounts.

CHAPTER 2

Key 1: Define Strategic Account Management as a Business Rather Than a Sales Initiative

This first key is the most critical. Embrace strategic account management as a way to improve your firm's overall business performance. When a supplier, as is common, defines strategic account management primarily as a sales initiative, the returns are limited. Everyone, not just sales, needs to own the strategic account. If other departments see account management only as a sales initiative, salespeople are likely to have an unrewarding, uphill battle.

The Federated story that precedes this chapter shows what can happen when sales alone owns the relationship, and other departments focus on their own issues. The other departments need to be on board because sales almost never delivers the offering; it depends on other functions' committed and coordinated efforts to create and deliver value. We have too often seen sales ask other departments to expend a great deal of effort—with no reward and possible penalties—to meet the strategic accounts' needs. When those departments have not been a part of creating the strategic account program or its goals, they may resist or even refuse sales' requests. In such cases, neither the customer nor the supplier wins. But both can win if strategic account management starts as a business rather than a sales initiative.

Doing so requires taking three important steps, which we will examine:

1. Create cross-functional executive leadership.
2. Understand and align around accounts' business challenges.
3. Start strategic account management programs as business initiatives.

CREATE CROSS-FUNCTIONAL EXECUTIVE LEADERSHIP

If a strategic account management program is going to be successful, the firm, ideally before program launch, must systematically identify and work with departments on whom they and the customers will rely. One successful means of doing so is to create a cross-functional executive group that can deal with any pre- and post-launch issues. Cross-functional executive leadership helps create and communicate the urgency that ensures organizational commitment.

Cross-functional executive leadership helps create and communicate the urgency that ensures organizational commitment.

In many cases, these executives make the financial case for serving strategic accounts differently and then, working with the other functional executives, create clear account management goals and objectives. These cross-functional meetings help sales and other departments arrive at shared priorities, delivery schedules, and service levels. Some suppliers even adjust their recognition and reward programs to recognize departments outside sales for participating in account management. The cross-functional executive team may reward manufacturing, for example, for balancing line utilization with one-off responsiveness to strategic accounts. The key is to keep the departments whole, at the very least, when they make special contributions to strategic account management.

When this internal alignment is driven by cross-functional executives before program launch, the firm can minimize the amount of internal selling account managers will do after program rollout. Alignment also means that multiple departments working together can deliver solutions much more quickly. In successful programs, we have often seen the initial cross-functional executive group continue to meet regularly as a steering committee for the strategic account program. The cross-functional executives can deal with a problem before it becomes a crisis. This executive steering committee can, in other words, ensure that sales' best deal is no longer manufacturing's worst nightmare.

If you already have strategic account management and wish to overcome some of the internal resistance you may be experiencing, consider backtracking by creating a cross-functional executive team to help you optimize your program.

UNDERSTAND AND ALIGN AROUND ACCOUNTS' BUSINESS CHALLENGES

Once strategic account management begins, it usually takes 3 to 12 months to understand the targeted customers' business challenges well enough to co-create value and sell strategic solutions. This is not to say you won't increase sales in the short term, but the real opportunity is to play big.

We know one strategic account manager at an energy-control firm who spent a good year learning the business of a large brewery. At the end of that time, she could discuss beer making with the master brewers and, through those discussions, she uncovered several processes that could achieve significant cost-savings with more efficient power usage. After she identified those opportunities, she worked with her internal manufacturing people to design and create the power-management control devices the brewery required. The account manager, then armed with a proposal that included cost and quantified value offered, approached the brewery decision makers, who quickly accepted her proposal.

Consider this supplier's selling situation: no RFPs and no competitors. A dedicated and determined account manager generated a custom solution that she knew met the customer's payback requirements. A committed and coordinated manufacturing group then delivered that solution. In most key account selling programs we know, the salesperson would not have been given this much time to produce results at an individual account. Strategic account management takes the longer view and, depending on the skills of the account manager, offers the greater payoff over time.

One reason the role of account managers can be so exciting and so challenging is that they have to know both the customer's business and their business in great depth. That takes time and persistence. When helping account managers take inventory of their account knowledge, we often use a five-page, 80-question self-test, focusing on:

1. The customer's organization.
2. The customer's suppliers.
3. The customer's customers.
4. The customer's competitors.
5. The customer's joint venture and
   alliance partners.
6. Your competitors for this account.

Answered carefully, the questions can generate opportunities for creative customer solutions. The self-test provides strategic account managers with the in-depth customer knowledge they need to produce long-term, high-payoff initiatives.

Let us now look at two firms that successfully implemented strategic account management as a business initiative: Honeywell Industrial Automation and Control Solutions and Minnesota Power.

START STRATEGIC ACCOUNT MANAGEMENT PROGRAMS AS BUSINESS INITIATIVES: HONEYWELL INDUSTRIAL AUTOMATION AND CONTROL SOLUTIONS

Honeywell Industrial Automation and Control Solutions (IACS) has a long, successful history of close working relationships with its key customers, most of whom are huge integrated oil and chemical companies. As those customers faced increasing competitive pressure and demand for higher financial returns in the mid-1990s, they pushed Honeywell to reduce costs, accelerate performance, provide global consistency, and demonstrate increased investment returns. Some customers instituted strategic sourcing programs designed to select one or two key suppliers for all future global automation investments.

Honeywell had been responding to these market demands tactically, on an account-by-account or project-by-project basis, which dramatically increased selling costs. Coupled with competitive pressure to discount prices, Honeywell's profit margins were severely squeezed.

Honeywell's challenge was to implement a process that strategically responded to the market demand, created sustained competitive advantage, and ensured long-term growth and profitability for both customer and Honeywell IACS. The program was profit-, strategy-, and process-based.

In 1996, Honeywell formed the Strategic Corporate Accounts Program to provide this systematic approach to strategic account management. Even its title refers back to the accounts' ownership: strategic *corporate* accounts. This program was and is focused on establishing strategic account management as a core competency within Honeywell IACS. The division began to create and implement consistent processes, bringing discipline to managing these strategic account relationships. Honeywell IACS's Strategic Corporate Accounts organization currently manages 11 global petrochemical and energy companies, representing some 35+ percent of Honeywell IACS's total global revenue.

Honeywell has a process-oriented culture. Instead of charging into an account management process, as many firms have done, Honeywell developed, with cross-functional help, a program vision, responsibilities, interdependencies, account selection criteria, and some very special dedicated resources to link Honeywell IACS (the firm) with strategic corporate accounts.

The vision for Honeywell's Strategic Corporate Accounts Program was "to create value through a world-class, relationship-centric strategic approach that complements Honeywell's technology leadership and differentiates its value from that of its competition." To support this vision, the Strategic Corporate Accounts Program has a number of responsibilities, including:

- Establish and manage strategic business relationships worldwide.
- Facilitate the global introduction, integration, and adoption of framework/processes.
- Measure and report the total value and ROI of Strategic Corporate Accounts.
- Communicate and coordinate internally and externally to achieve organizational alignment, ensure consistency, and transfer knowledge regarding strategic relationship development and management.

We have chosen these four responsibilities because sales alone cannot accomplish them. These tasks require the coordinated efforts of many folks in many Honeywell functions on many continents.

When strategic corporate accounts went after accounts, they looked for customers who:

- valued automation as strategic investment that produces competitive advantage;
- showed a commitment to Honeywell IACS as a strategic first-choice supplier;
- were strategically aligned with Honeywell IACS;
- were willing to create a joint value proposition;
- were globally positioned, with clear global requirements and a desire for global consistency; and
- merited an investment in a strategic relationship, which included:
  - a relationship manager;
  - a senior executive champion;
  - an executive steering committee; and
  - technology interaction

Honeywell used these criteria—and others—to begin distinguishing customers meriting a strategic corporate approach. And while sales might do some of the research, achieving strategic alignment and making a business case for a potential strategic corporate account takes a significant time investment by numerous functions beyond sales.

To support the strategic corporate account activities, Honeywell IACS created a cross-functional support group that combined competencies in Strategic Businesses, Business Process, Technology Alignment, and global linkages. Honeywell IACS believed the key to a successful strategic corporate accounts program was balancing the need for a common and consistent account management process with a structure that accommodated the unique, value-differentiating needs of each specific customer.

Honeywell created two functions—Business Resources and Technology Alignment—to support the common elements of the account management process.

The Business Resource team develops and manages the framework and processes to manage IACS's strategic business relationships. This team provides overall support for Strategic Corporate Accounts, including: business planning, identification and application of internal and external best practices, and Strategic Corporate Account organization communication and reporting to the other business units.

Honeywell IACS believed the key to a successful strategic corporate accounts program was balancing the need for a common and consistent account management process with a structure that accommodated the unique, value-differentiating needs of each specific customer.

Another common element to all Honeywell IACS's strategic relationships is the customers' desire to achieve competitive advantage through automation. The Strategic Technology Alignment function ensures that the solutions Honeywell IACS develops do, in fact, meet the specific, prioritized needs of its strategic accounts. The technology alignment function also ensures those solutions realize superior value for both Honeywell IACS and the customer. Technology Alignment communicates the strategic corporate account's technology requirements to any Honeywell Strategic Business Unit that is helping craft a solution for that customer. In addition, the function supports planning technology directions, resolves common technology issues, and quantifies value propositions for technology applications in Strategic Corporate Accounts.

For managing the unique elements of each strategic relationship, every Strategic Corporate Account has a full-time, dedicated business manager with a dedicated support team and defined global linkages. These business managers are accountable for the pro-forma global P&L of each strategic relationship. These managers also support framework/process implementation and continuous improvement within assigned account relationships.

Honeywell IACS is currently moving toward a Six Sigma approach to account relationship management. Traditionally a tool to lessen variation in manufacturing, Six Sigma potentially will allow Honeywell IACS to achieve the next level of excellence in strategic/global account management. And Honeywell realizes that sales alone will not be able to control all the potential variables in managing a strategic corporate relationship, such as establishing and managing parallel linkages between all critical functions at the supplier and account. To create firmwide relationships, Honeywell worldwide must work together to continually meet and exceed the targeted accounts' expectations.

This story started with high costs of sales and lessened profitability. What impact has the strategic corporate accounts program had on Honeywell IACS? Between 1997 and 1999, Honeywell IACS:

The Honeywell IACS Strategic Corporate Accounts Program demonstrates positive business results achievable when a firm's multiple functions re-engineer the supplier-customer interface.

- Reduced overall selling cost by 40 percent.

- Grew 61 percent in a flat-to-declining business environment.

- Increased annual per-strategic account manager sales productivity by 100 percent.

- Improved divisional profitability by 20 percent.

During 1995–97, Honeywell IACS also reduced some customers' per-project service costs by 15 to 30 percent. One example: Honeywell IACS developed an automation co-sourcing option for procuring instruments for a strategic corporate account's plant, a $250 million project in which the account received huge annual benefits: $60 million in yield benefits, $9 million in reliability improvements, and a $20 million after-tax incremental cash flow, beginning in the first year.

Our conclusion? The Honeywell IACS Strategic Corporate Accounts Program demonstrates positive business results achievable when a firm's multiple functions re-engineer the supplier-customer interface.

When a supplier like Honeywell IACS sets out to institutionalize alliance behavior across the organizational boundaries of the business relationship, it removes barriers, shares information, develops trust, and enables both supplier and customer to achieve superior business results.

THE MINNESOTA POWER STORY

Electric utilities have seldom been held out as examples of customer focus, which makes the story of Minnesota Power (MP), a utility in Duluth, all the more extraordinary. In the mid-nineties the U.S. power market started to change as signs were increasing that deregulation of power was imminent. While most utilities could see that they were going to have to do business in a very different way, MP was one of the few utilities to aggressively start realigning its culture to serve its most critical customers.

DRIVERS FOR MINNESOTA POWER'S STRATEGIC ACCOUNT REALIGNMENT

In 1994 the majority of MP's largest customer contracts were ending in the next few years. Steve Sherner, MP's vice president of Large Power Marketing, heard rumblings from these customers that they would not sign up again unless the contracts' terms were more flexible to their needs. As one customer executive put it, "MP needs to wake up and understand the beast they're serving—what it takes for us to survive long term.

Our survival is their future." Other large power customers went beyond rumbling. One of them petitioned the Minnesota Public Utilities Commission, asking that they be allowed to get their power from a local cooperative rather than from MP. The account lost. Another account sought open access from the legislature so customers could get power from anywhere they wanted. That bill was denied by only one vote in the Minnesota senate.

The large-customer rumblings then grew louder and clearer. After its new short-term contract was signed in 1995, MP's single largest customer ($45+ million a year) refused to come celebrate with MP because it felt there was nothing to celebrate. Later, in the spring of 1995, Sherner commissioned assessments on the firm's largest power customers. He wanted an objective third-party view of these relationships to test his concerns and to make certain MP executives heard directly from strategic accounts. Shortly into this assessment, MP confirmed that this account's executives were very dissatisfied with the MP relationship. Account contacts were eloquent about embracing the future of deregulation: they were actively looking for a new power supplier. Those conducting the account assessments strongly suggested that MP mount a major effort to repair this large-customer relationship.

WHAT KEY PLAYERS DID TO STRATEGICALLY REALIGN MINNESOTA POWER

Besides the market shift, contract expirations, and large-customer complaints, the fourth driver in realigning the corporate culture was the addition of two new players at MP. The utility named Ed Russell, from outside MP and the utility industry, as corporate CEO. MP also promoted Bob Edwards, its very creative CFO, to president. Russell knew about business and customers but had little experience with utilities and so, while staying closely involved, he allowed Bob Edwards to lead that part of the business.

On one of their very first days on the job, Russell and Edwards attended the presentation of the large-customer assessments. Hearing about how their largest customers felt about MP was certainly not the happiest way to begin their tenures. But both Russell and Edwards saw the customer feedback as a gift and said it presented an opportunity for MP to protect and develop its critical relationship assets.

Eric Norberg, then director of Large Power Marketing, emerged at this point to take a leadership role in assisting both in the relationship repair and corporate alignment. Norberg oversaw the large-power relationships, working closely with two seasoned account managers, Dave Lundein and Brad Oachs. Norberg, Lundein, and Oachs assumed a more proactive role in the relationships and negotiations, working to make contracts more flexible for MP's largest customers. As so many others at MP did, they rose to the challenges in front of them.

On April 25, 1996, Norberg held a meeting of MP executives and managers to develop the repair strategy for the largest account. All those at the meeting stepped up and assumed strategic responsibility for managing the repair effort. As Norberg said, "(W)ith industry restructuring coming, we really didn't want to lose (the largest account's) contract (or any contract for that matter). In fact we were committed to using the results of that contract as a cornerstone of our restructuring effort for the company."

To further this relationship building and contract negotiation, Edwards met personally with the largest customer's general manager in Minnesota. Each left his lawyers and support people behind, which made negotiation much easier. After the GM and Edwards defined their interests and concerns, Edwards brought those issues back to MP staff so they could create customer solutions. As the GM said, "It was a good move by Bob. He took a big risk, though, because if it didn't work out with us, he had no line of appeal left at MP." For the first time, the general manager could see that MP was serious about listening to his plant's needs.

After the April meeting, Norberg assumed tactical control of the largest account's relationship-repair process, managing the multiple relationships between people in MP departments and parallel functions at the customer. Edwards, Norberg, and

MP's other decision makers had a major insight at this point—that the large-power marketing department alone could not drive MP's alignment around strategic accounts. If the alignment were not supported by the other functions, one customer phone call to an old-mindset MP employee might jeopardize that account relationship—however large. Norberg does admit, though, that MP's cultural realignment to strategic relationship management was made easier by MP's values. "Minnesota nice" is much more than an expression. Employees wanted to have good relationships with customers and see them succeed. Now management had aggressively given them such an opportunity.

Norberg began breaking down MP's functional walls. He made certain that all parties within MP who would have to implement a contract were consulted and on board before any deals were struck. He also kept these same people in the loop whenever a customer meeting or communication occurred. His basic responsibility was making sure that MP lived up to its commitments. Norberg's team included some 30 cross-functional MP employees. He worked with them to gather ideas, to figure out how to work the regulations in the customers' favor, and how to reinforce Russell's and Edwards' original message about protecting and developing critical relationship assets.

INITIAL SUCCESSES IN MINNESOTA POWER'S STRATEGIC REALIGNMENT

MP's results in relationship repair were impressive. In mid-1996, the experts were saying that power deregulation in Minnesota was no more than two to three years off. Utility customers around the country were challenging contracts; some were breaking them. But at MP months of work in relationship management, alignment, and collaborative negotiation began to pay off. In August, MP and its largest customer agreed to a new precedent-setting, 11-year service agreement, which then had to be accepted by the Minnesota Public Utilities Commission.

In November of 1996, when it became clear that MP's 18 months of work had paid off, Eric Norberg held a celebratory dinner for his 30-member relationship-repair team. At one point Norberg had the entire group stand in a circle, recognized people by name, and read their contributions to the repair process. Norberg then gave each employee a plaque that had a newspaper headline mentioning him or her by name, followed by a story that celebrated each person's role in turning the relationship around. It was a celebration and appreciation of all the efforts of the team members. We consider this public recognition a best practice in both relationship repair and strategic-realignment work.

The success became official on December 23, 1996, when the Minnesota Public Utilities Commission approved the MP-customer contract. MP's competitors—those firms seeking to supply power to MP's largest accounts—were floored, both by the agreement and by its length. At that point, with deregulation looming, virtually no large-power customer was signing a long-term contract.

In mid-1997, Norberg wanted to ensure that MP would learn from its past. He commissioned a learning history about the repair of its largest customer relationship. The learning history captured all the key steps in the MP-account relationship as well as critical decisions, victories, and mistakes. The learning history was used to train MP executives and staff and to identify other potential high-risk account relationships.

Bob Edwards held a critical meeting in the fall of 1997 at Bluefin, Minnesota. Almost everyone to whom we spoke singled Bluefin out as a milestone in his or her MP career. Thirty MP leaders, led by two outside facilitators, met to map out MP's new strategic direction. Looking back at that meeting, Edwards says, "We saw that for our company to be successful, we had to work with customers, whether we were regulated or not. Based on these insights, we flipped the organizational chart, putting customers at the top, and decided what we were going to be doing in the next 10 years. I had attended many brainstorming meetings that never led to anything so I was not looking forward to this meeting. But Bluefin was structured in such a way that the communication was of a very different sort. The discussions were very candid. Together key MP areas and managers identified our current strengths and weaknesses. . . . We then decided what we were going to do . . . and, just as critically, what we were *not* going to do. We closed offices, consolidated our efforts, stopped selling nonpower products, and stopped accepting projects below a certain dollar level. We identified the MP activities that were basically distractions from where we wanted to go—even if they seemed to offer a big payoff."

"What I remember especially about that meeting was that we had scheduled it for two days, a Wednesday and a Thursday. After two days we saw we would need more time and every single participant agreed to meet again—not grudgingly—because they could see that our decisions were going to reshape the company. I'll always remember that; it was so different from a traditional utility's 8 to 5 commitment." Dave McMillan, then an MP corporate lawyer with a commitment to customer relationships, recalls that Bluefin "fundamentally changed the way we did business."

MINNESOTA POWER REALIGNS AROUND CRITICAL CUSTOMERS

After MP mapped out its direction at Bluefin, Edwards reinforced his message yet again, this time by restructuring and staffing MP to meet the needs of its large customers. Edwards promoted Eric Norberg to vice president of Strategic Accounts, which sent a strong message to MP and to its customers. He named Bob Adams VP of Finance and Dave McMillan VP of Customer Solutions, an entirely new department set up to support strategic accounts. As McMillan recalls, "We were set up to provide Eric and the Strategic Accounts group with one-stop shopping. If they needed analytical help or regulatory help or anything to do a deal, we had the people ready to help them. We no longer wanted them to have to go through many departments to get things done. We'd help them price things out, coordinate any necessary commission filing—such as released energy. I think this (restructuring) was a brilliant move on the part of Bob Edwards." Edwards had created the infrastructure that allowed MP's strategic account managers to focus on their assigned customers. And Adams, Norberg, and McMillan formed a team that communicated and coordinated very effectively. This ensured that the large customers would receive the best that MP had to offer and that the customer-focused message continued circulating throughout the organization.

In the first quarter of 1998, Edwards took his message to virtually all the MP employees—in groups of 10 to 50—explaining the new strategy, how it was arrived at, what MP hoped to accomplish, and taking questions. If there had been any doubts as to MP's strategic direction, they were now cleared up. Everyone at MP was moving in the same direction—toward meeting the needs of strategic accounts.

WHY MINNESOTA POWER SUCCEEDED AT STRATEGIC REALIGNMENT

We asked those at MP why the three-year alignment and restructuring around customers had been so successful when so many other firms had failed in similar endeavors. The MP employees told us that there were several reasons. First and foremost was that the charge had been led by Bob Edwards, who made his position known and who then staffed and changed the organization to support that position. As Dave McMillan says, "There was no way a lesser executive could have pulled this off." But it wasn't just positional power that made Edwards effective. It was, as McMillan says, "that (Edwards) showed how much of a personal commitment he wanted to make by laying out the new strategy for every employee in the company."

Another reason for success was that virtually everyone at MP stepped up to the challenge the firm was facing, assuming personal responsibility to find solutions. At the same time, MP's drive toward strategic alignment was data-driven, from the customer assessments to the very unpleasant financial cases developed to show what would happen should MP continue doing business as usual. And just as critical was Edwards' and Norberg's early realization that change could not be driven solely by marketing; all functional areas needed to be a part of the effort. This led the company to develop a number of cross-functional teams who scored successes by working together in entirely new ways. That realization also led to the creation of the Strategic Accounts department as well as the Customer Solutions group. Most critically, it led to new communication processes that meant every MP employee could keep up with the strategy and what was happening with the largest accounts.

As Bob Edwards says, "For us, alignment wasn't just a program—a flavor of the day. . . . (W)hat we launched is first and foremost what we are doing today. We truly transformed the culture. I feel best about that. You wouldn't hear a different story if you asked anyone at MP what we did then and what is really important to us now. Our goals are now inbred in the organization—and not just in the marketing groups but in all functions." Strategic account management was not a sales initiative. Instead, it was an organizational and cultural initiative, changing MP's business model.

Most firms we know started strategic account management programs as sales initiatives, creating what were essentially key account selling programs. Key account selling can be an effective way to generate increased customer revenues. Our experience has been, however, that getting firm buy-in and commitment prior to rolling out strategic account management can take those account relationships and their revenues to a level far beyond those achieved by key account selling. Successful strategic account management programs tend to start by creating committed and coordinated cross-departmental executive support groups behind the account management process. These groups lessen the internal marketing the strategic account manager must do, freeing him to focus on managing and growing the relationship. The cross-functional groups, working within an account management process, also tend to lower the overall costs of sales, especially when they redesign existing processes to serve strategic accounts. Finally, creating and managing the internal relationships required to serve strategic accounts allows the supplier, as we saw with Minnesota

Power, to chip away at cultural and functional cross-company issues that limit a firm's overall competitiveness and ROA.

> **If . . . it takes a village to raise a child, it takes an entire firm to own and manage a strategic account relationship.**

Not aligning all functions in the service of strategic accounts will, in many cases, create a situation such as the one we saw with the Federated story just before Chapter 1. If, as the African proverb goes, it takes a village to raise a child, it takes an entire firm to own and manage a strategic account relationship.

DEFINE STRATEGIC ACCOUNT MANAGEMENT AS A BUSINESS RATHER THAN A SALES INITIATIVE

How can you ensure that strategic account management will be a firm initiative?

1. The firm's senior leadership must see the financial sense of treating customers as strategic accounts.
2. All key departments need to be heading in roughly the same direction. The supplier's cross-functional executives and managers must work together from program design to program implementation and, ideally, after program launch.
3. Departments outside sales must be recognized for their contributions to strategic account management.

Key 2: Create Firm Alignment and Commitment to Meet Strategic Accounts' Needs and Expectations

In Chapter 1, we examined firms that realized the potential of account management because they approached it as a business initiative—a means of optimizing business performance—rather than as a pure sales initiative. In this chapter, we look at other companies that, by defining customer management as a business strategy, were then able to align and mobilize their organizations to implement that strategy. Organizational alignment works when firms gain their employees' commitment and thus energize them to serve accounts more effectively. This chapter examines methods that have helped companies achieve such alignment, in the hope that you might apply similar approaches to your firm.

There are four sections to this chapter:

1. What is organizational alignment?
2. What are the benefits of organizational alignment?
3. What makes organizational alignment difficult?
4. How can a firm create organizational alignment?

WHAT IS ORGANIZATIONAL ALIGNMENT?— THREE CRITICAL ELEMENTS

For us, organizational alignment means getting every department and employee headed in roughly the same direction, concentrating their power. Peter Senge says the difference between focused and unfocused organizational power is the difference between a light bulb, which throws out scattered light, and a laser, where light is so concentrated that it can cut through steel.[1] Organizational alignment offers that kind of focused power for companies and their most critical customers.

We can cite a near-universal example of diffuse versus concentrated power in strategic account management. In almost every firm, account managers hand off tasks to other departments. What happens after that hand-off differentiates between the aligned/focused and the unaligned/unfocused organizations. If, perhaps through bitter experience, the strategic account manager doubts that the employee accepting the handoff really understands the task's urgency, she is forced to either follow that individual around or call periodically to make sure that the job gets done. This is not a value-added task for the strategic account manager, except to the extent that it ensures the task gets completed.

Every minute account managers spend making up for an unaligned organization is a minute that could be used to uncover new opportunities for mutual value.

Compare that to a firm such as Marriott International, whose story appears below, in which virtually all employees stand ready—as a "volunteer army"—to assist strategic accounts. Here the account manager hands off the task to the account team and moves on to his next task, secure that the job will get done. Every minute account managers spend making up for an

---

[1]   Senge, Peter (1990). *The Fifth Discipline: the Art & Practice of the Learning Organization* (p.234). New York: Currency Books.

unaligned organization is a minute that could be used to un-cover new opportunities for mutual value. The true costs of the unaligned firm are the lost opportunity costs that keep the firm from realizing its true bottom-line potential.

F I G U R E 3–1

Three Elements of Organizational Alignment

---

1. A common vision and set of values.

2. Systematic and ongoing communication of that vision and values.

3. Structural changes.

---

1. A Common Vision and Set of Values

The first element of alignment is a *common vision* or picture of where the company and the strategic account group are headed. This picture not only keeps the end state in mind but it also helps employees determine their priorities and make good decisions in ambiguous times. It helps provide the rationale for why groups need to work together and it focuses people on the big picture so they can find common ground. The values guide employees to achieve the vision.

This picture/vision is often most effectively generated by a multilevel cross-functional leadership group, using objective market and customer data. Because the group will articulate the vision in words, it is important to let them wrestle with a common understanding of what the words mean. This requires more than talking. It requires a skillful dialog between people and departments that will lead to the understanding and com-mitment that organizational alignment requires. Honeywell Industrial Automation & Control people, for example, believe their success is driven by their mission, which in 1999 was "to create value through a world-class, relationship-centric strate-gic approach that complements Honeywell's technology lead-ership and differentiates its value from that of its competition."

2. Systematic and Ongoing Communication of That Vision and Values

The second component of alignment is *systematic and ongoing communication—both from the customer and deep within the organization*. This communication should reinforce why the firm has chosen to move toward its vision. As noted in the Introduction and Chapter 1, this directional focus is quite different from the multiple and internal focuses that dominate many firms. Objective customer data—gathered in many ways—allows the vision to complement the marketing strategy. Successful leaders and their companies, such as Bob Edwards of Minnesota Power, invest enormous time and resources ensuring the quality and effectiveness of the communications process. Skillful leaders repeat key messages to help focus all employees on the vision and the near-term goals to achieve it.

Communication processes that pull (not push) the vision throughout the organization provide a way to introduce and reinforce the vision, to detail the responsibilities the vision creates, and to present how well people are performing in those responsibilities. Such processes do not magically appear. They must be carefully crafted and used if the vision is going to stay in the forefront of employees' efforts. A firm seeking to align itself needs to develop systematic communication plans and processes to make key messages travel to all departments and levels of an organization.

3. Structural Changes

Traditionally, firms tend to define alignment primarily as a *structural issue:* restructuring reporting relationships. Our experience, however, has been that restructuring without a clear vision and strong communication support will be a wasted effort. Some firms then focus on redesigning those processes serving internal and external customers. Process redesign and organizational restructuring are certainly major parts of alignment. Our experience, however, has been that unless the restructuring follows the agreed-upon vision, restructuring for alignment tends to fail.

We have seen well-intentioned companies allocate large budgets for setting up and staffing a strategic management function and then have no money left for planning, support, training, or internal marketing. They believed that creating the department would be enough. Because strategic account management is a very different way of working with customers, though, these programs often fail through lack of support.

The goal of strategic account management is to work smarter, not harder. Without a vision, departments and their employees will continue to follow their own directions. Without systematic communication processes that promote the voice of the customer and the goals of the organization, developing that vision can easily turn into an academic exercise. Without work process redesign/reengineering, employees might know of the vision but will not move toward achieving it in the most effective way. In our experience, firms cannot work smarter unless all three of these elements are addressed simultaneously.

The goal of strategic account management is to work smarter, not harder.

WHAT ARE THE BENEFITS OF ALIGNMENT?

F I G U R E   3–2

Benefits of Alignment

1. Improved performance.
2. Greater account satisfaction.
3. Greater focus and momentum.
4. Increased efficiency.
5. More time to spend on adding value.
6. Greater employee satisfaction.

Aligned firms, such as Honeywell Industrial Automation & Control Solutions or Minnesota Power, ultimately reduced costs through more collaborative customer and supplier relationships. When the firm is committed to the strategy, it will take significantly less time—and fewer resources—to get things done. Processes and systems will take care of all that can be systematized; increased employee urgency will cover those actions not appropriate for process redesign.

In *Getting Partnering Right*, Neil Rackham et al. present the Motorola-United Parcel Service case, in which Motorola found itself "too slow to respond to the changing needs of customers, who increasingly were moving to just-in-time manufacturing and reducing their inventories. Customers were demanding faster shipments but they didn't expect to pay premium rates to get them."[2] Motorola decided to find a distribution partner who could work closely with it to create a new process.

It chose UPS, which created a more effective, aligned shipping process with Motorola and immediately created a 60+ percent savings in shipping time by cutting out wasteful steps in the shipping process. Sharing data further cut costs "by reducing the re-keying of shipping information and eliminating duplication in customs documentation and other paperwork."[3] As the partnership has grown, more than 60 percent of products were shipped direct, "so Motorola has been able to dismantle some of its own high-overhead distribution infrastructure,[4] which resulted in greater cost savings.

At this point, UPS was not selling shipping; it was selling one of its core competencies: logistics. One way of defining a core competency is the ability to bring expertise and aligned processes to bear on a customer problem.

But reduced costs are not the only potential benefit for the aligned supplier. Increased alignment means greater employee

---

[2]   Rackham, N., et al. (1996). *Getting Partnering Right: How Market Leaders Are Creating Long-Term Competitive Advantage* (p. 59). New York, McGraw-Hill.
[3]   Ibid, p.59.
[4]   Ibid, p.60

satisfaction and loyalty. Employees get to spend time on important tasks rather than on constant rework. They can make better, more informed decisions because their priorities are clear. Because everyone has recognized that they are responsible for account satisfaction and loyalty, everyone becomes part of the firm's value offering. For many—if not most—employees, being part of important work, adding value, and making a difference are critical motivators.

A core competency is the ability to bring expertise and aligned processes to bear on a customer problem.

Aligned suppliers minimize internal bottlenecks that could have undermined relationships. That frees them to spend more time "mining" for opportunities to increase account share. Employees at such firms tend spend less time worrying about covering their own inefficiencies and more time focusing on the accounts' needs. They can really listen to the account contacts. If you have ever had anyone make the effort to really listen to you, you know what a profound experience it can be.

Once employees really hear customers, then your firm suddenly has many customer champions looking for business problems, solutions, and ways to co-create value. And as they create joint value, the relationship tends to get better and better, and the customer tends to grow more and more loyal—no matter how volatile the market. Think of Honeywell IACS's 61 percent growth in a flat-to-declining market. In our experience, selling competencies is almost always a higher-margin sale than selling standard offerings. Alignment helps the bottom line grow while offering real power to differentiate, particularly because alignment is so difficult to achieve. But those firms that do align with customers tend to be market leaders—such as Johnson & Johnson, Honeywell Industrial Automation & Control Solutions, and Marriott International.

WHAT MAKES ALIGNMENT SO DIFFICULT?

Before we look at specific companies' approaches to alignment, let's consider why it is so difficult to gain organizational commitment to an account management strategy. When we create organizations, we tend to reflect our humanity. Organizations, like people, tend to be inherently selfish. We—and our firms—tend to worry most about how things affect us directly, how we can be recognized, and how we can avoid frustration and confusion. It is, therefore, often more important for us to please our boss, who directly determines our raises, rather than pleasing the customer, whom we may never see. Because of those priorities, it is sometimes easier for us to see account requests as nuisances.

We tend to prefer predictability over change, so we create processes to make things more predictable. And, anyway, companies are always trying some new management program or strategy. Many employees believe that if they keep their head down long enough, account management, like other programs, will just blow away, until it gets replaced by some new program, which will also blow away. Many employees undoubtedly wish that their CEO would stop reading management books.

There is some exaggeration here, but not much. Alignment's first challenge is getting executives from many departments to create the common vision, which ideally speaks to a firm's largest customer relationships. Creating this vision requires strong dialog skills, something often lacking in management teams. The team requires strong trust among the team members so people can safely and productively disagree. It requires that management focus as much on the process of working together to create a vision as they do on the task itself. And because few management teams function this effectively, great visions that generate enthusiasm and commitment are hard to come by. Great visions require hard work and soul searching, but the payoff in terms of organizational performance is huge.

Once a company communicates the vision, its second challenge is permeating that message throughout the company and translating that vision into specific tasks. Vision builders need to present why the firm has chosen the vision so employees become committed to that direction. It's the most challenging kind of sale—one that asks people to do their work differently and to reframe their definitions of "account" and "success."

The company must reinforce its commitment to that vision again and again, a vigilant reinforcement that is exceedingly tough. One firm we know actually started measuring the amounts of time executives spent visiting and speaking to customers. Other firms recognize people for their commitment to the vision. Several of these firms have extra-mile clubs, in which employees receive recognition and sometimes prizes for having gone the extra mile in helping customers. These employees see to it that their company tracks down a strategic account order, solves a problem, or answers a question in a timely manner.

Implementing the vision requires creativity, internal sales skills, high levels of accountability, the right accounts, and constant reinforcement. Each of these items requires tremendous self- and organizational discipline, a particularly challenging requirement at a time when a firm's short-term bottom line can rule. In too many firms, "the urgent drives out the important."[5] We have seen companies in which one executive destroyed great visions and relationships by making a short-term resources decision with a strategic account. Consider the sales executive who scrapped long-term program goals by offering huge incentive bonuses for exceeding one quarter's sales forecast. Strategic account management was essentially put on hold, customer relationships weakened as it became increasingly difficult to reach account executives, and the firm's commitment to the program withered.

---

[5] Hamel, G. and C. K. Prahalad (1994). *Competing for the Future: Breakthrough Strategies for Seizing Control of Your Industry and Creating the Markets of Tomorrow* (p. 4). Cambridge: Harvard Business School Press.

HOW CAN A FIRM CREATE ORGANIZATIONAL ALIGNMENT?

1. How Account Aligned Is Your Firm?

Let's start with a checklist we generated by analyzing several hundred interviews with lost accounts. We have given the checklist to several thousand account managers and directors of account management programs. Those who have taken it generally identify processes and systems to improve. The checklist *always* leads to productive discussion.

HOW ACCOUNT ALIGNED IS YOUR FIRM?[6]

FIGURE 3–3

How Account Aligned Is Your Firm?

		Strongly Disagree						Strongly Agree
1.	My firm defines strategic account relationships as its most valuable assets and defines resource allocations toward them as investments rather than costs.	1	2	3	4	5	6	7
2.	My firm has numerous financial, nonfinancial, and long-term goals for its strategic account management program—such as incremental revenue, developing account profiles, plans, retention, account share, satisfaction, loyalty, etc.	1	2	3	4	5	6	7
3.	My firm makes sure that every employee with any strategic account contact is account-focused, i.e., understands his/her marketing role and is ready/able to take responsibility for solving account problems.	1	2	3	4	5	6	7
4.	To minimize inconsistent communication and unreliability, my firm captures and communicates all commitments made to strategic accounts and tracks its performance regarding those commitments.	1	2	3	4	5	6	7
5.	My firm makes sure our account managers manage no more than 40–60 total personal relationships at strategic accounts.	1	2	3	4	5	6	7

[6] ©S4 Consulting, Inc.

F I G U R E 3–3 (Continued)

How Account Aligned is Your Firm?

		Strongly Disagree						Strongly Agree
6.	My firm's account managers have identified those strategic account contacts with whom they are incompatible and have designated another team member to manage those relationships.	1	2	3	4	5	6	7
7.	My firm's strategic account listening and feedback systems are sophisticated enough to give us adequate warning when an account contact is about to change.	1	2	3	4	5	6	7
8.	My firm recognizes how disruptive it is to change a strategic account contact, so we have developed recovery strategies to minimize the negative impact on the relationship when such a change happens.	1	2	3	4	5	6	7
9.	We measure our performance with strategic accounts based on standards that account contacts have defined.	1	2	3	4	5	6	7
10.	My firm's internal systems and processes are all focused on exceeding strategic account expectations rather than on the ease and efficiency of internal processing.	1	2	3	4	5	6	7
11.	During our recent size change (growth or downsizing), we carefully examined any negative strategic account impact before we removed/added people or changed any process.	1	2	3	4	5	6	7
12.	Because our size has been changing, we have established strategic account delivery standards that tell us when processes are starting to get overburdened, unresponsive, or underutilized.	1	2	3	4	5	6	7
13.	Our market listening and feedback system is sophisticated enough to identify and leverage any technological breakthrough in our industry.	1	2	3	4	5	6	7
14.	Our research and development sets the industry standard.	1	2	3	4	5	6	7
	Total Score							

Some observations on final scores. No matter who fills this checklist out—line workers, managers, VPs of sales, or CEOs—the vast majority of people rate their organization at 56 or below. That score signals major developmental opportunities. A 56 means an average rating of 4 for each question, a score we see as neutral. In the case of critical customers, this score means danger—your accounts have no particular reason to leave you; neither do they have any particular reason to stay.

Comparing scores by various internal groups can be particularly interesting. How does management's perception differ from that of the line? How does customer service's perceptions differ from those of sales? How does manufacturing's/operations' perception differ from that of sales? Looking at the scores from multiple perspectives provides opportunities for rich dialog and insights.

2. Review Your Strategies

Think about your corporate and strategic account management strategies. Then answer the following questions:

F I G U R E   3–4

Strategy Questions

1. Could someone deep in the organization explain your corporate and strategic account management strategies?

2. Do you have a written strategy for strategic accounts?

3. Are the end points of the strategies clear?

4. Will your average worker be able to use those strategies to make decisions and prioritize tasks?

5. Do people know what your firm is not going to do?

If you answer "no" to any of these questions, you have some major tasks ahead of you.

3. Drive the Voice of the Customer Deep Into the Organization

If you are aligning your organization around the customer, the voice of the customer needs to be loud and clear throughout the organization. There are a number of ways to do this.

Some companies—such as Nationwide Retirement Services (NRS), a strategic business unit of Nationwide Financial Services—have begun a "Voice of the Customer" Program. On a regular and proactive basis, NRS features customers through on-site visits, customer-focused newsletters, fun facts, anything that helps employees better understand what it is like to walk in the customer's shoes.

As Karen Eisenbach, a senior VP at NRS says, "We were so focused on doing our jobs that many employees forgot the reason we were working so hard. We needed an outside-in approach to get and keep everyone focused on the customer. Although you certainly can get that perspective from field personnel and customer satisfaction surveys, there is nothing as powerful as having the customer address your employees directly and making certain that—in a variety of ways—the customer is a living and breathing part of what you do everyday."[7] By bringing the customer's voice inside the building, NRS has been able to show employees that, while Nationwide cuts their checks, the customers pay their salary.

Gathering objective customer data in as many ways as possible to validate the findings is another powerful way to drive organizational change and alignment. Methods to collect such data include traditional market research, third-party account assessments, satisfaction surveys, and analyzing ongoing customer complaints and requests.

Market research is the most popular and certainly one of the most effective ways to get customer information. We will see below how Knauf Fiberglass creatively gathered customer data by using focus groups and surveys, classic marketing research tools.

---

[7] E-mail from Karen Eisenbach, November 15, 2002.

Third-party account assessments are another powerful and objective way to gauge how the relationship is working and to identify opportunities for account planning. Such assessments should be conducted with carefully designed instruments and face-to-face interviews. It has always amazed us that executives who will not fill out a 10-minute satisfaction survey will give you 60 to 90 minutes for an interview. The primary purpose of these account assessments is to more objectively hear accounts' hopes, concerns, and expectations. The assessments emphasize the customers' strategy and business challenges and how the supplier can most easily help accounts achieve their business objectives.

In these interviews, skilled questioners also ask multiple account contacts to rate both their service- and relationship-quality expectations and how well the supplier is performing against these expectations. The interview data the questioners generate includes quantitative analysis of those ratings and, more critically, detailed customer stories that explain those ratings. Analyzing this data is one of the most robust ways of unearthing the drivers of account loyalty. The ultimate benefit of this approach is that not only do you get valuable information, but you reinforce the relationship by demonstrating through your investment how much you value customers and their opinions.

Perhaps the best executive case made for strategic account assessments comes from Bob Protzman, former vice president of marketing at Schneider National, the world's largest transportation company. When Protzman spoke at the Conference Board's 1998 Relationship Management Conference, he described some of the reasons that he hired a third party to interview the company's critical accounts systematically:

> First, you will get dispassionate, objective observers who are well trained and seasoned interviewers. They know what questions to ask and, sometimes more important, how to ask them. And they're not inclined to start disagreeing with the customer by defending themselves when the customer begins to criticize us. That's very hard for your own people to refrain from doing.

Remember, you need to define reality on the basis of the customer's perceptions—not your own.

Second, customers are much more likely to be up front and honest with an information broker than they are with you. We continually get information from these interviews that we have never heard before, and we're talking to these people all the time!

Third, the customer is really impressed when you call in third parties to get to the bottom of a relationship problem. Clearly, it nails one problem that is almost always at the heart of troubled relationships—the perception that you don't care. . . . One of those [customers] was one of the largest home center retailers, and this intervention by outside professionals was necessary to get a meaningful dialog going with them.

I still remember the Key Account Assessment report on the paper manufacturer. . . . Although the [numbers] on satisfaction weren't terrible, the qualitative feedback was a wake-up call regarding many of the soft issues. Advice and contextual information like this is vitally important, and there is no way we could have come up with most of this on our own."[8]

Protzman effectively provides the rationale for third-party strategic account assessments, but knowing strategic relationships' service- and relationship-quality expectations is not enough. The supplier will then ideally improve those areas where it is not performing to expectations—the process redesign mentioned earlier.

Below is the story of Knauf Fiberglass, a firm that creatively and systematically learned its major customers' expectations, and then used the data to align internal departments and make major performance improvements. The Knauf Fiberglass story presents all three of our alignment elements: creating a vision, developing better communication approaches with customers and within the firm, and redesigning processes that serve both the internal and external customer.

---

[8] Taken from a presentation by Bob Protzman at the 1998 Conference Board's Conference on Relationship Management.

KNAUF FIBERGLASS CASE—VIDEO FOCUS GROUPS AND EMPLOYEE SWAT TEAMS

Knauf Fiberglass, headquartered in Shelbyville, Indiana, makes insulation and other building products for residential and industrial/commercial applications. Knauf's strategic accounts are its distributors. In the early 1990s, Knauf began to get rumblings from these distributors about product and service quality issues. Knauf executives, though, did not want to allocate resources for fixing things until they could prioritize their largest distributors' expectations, needs, and what they thought needed to be fixed.

Knauf arranged for six videotaped focus groups (two each in three locations across the United States) to assess its critical distributor relationships. The focus groups helped determine (1) what distributors expected from a world-class fiberglass manufacturer, (2) which Knauf/distributor interactions were critical, and (3) which of Knauf's interactions it performed effectively and which Knauf did not perform well. At this point, Knauf had 12 hours of raw customer video, much of which Knauf executives watched. Knauf then had a 50+ question, in-depth survey designed, based on the critical distributors' needs and expectations—as stated in the video focus groups.

Jeff Brisley, vice president of residential sales, managed the distributor assessment project in a way that helped Knauf's culture become more aligned on the distributors' needs. Historically, Knauf suffered from the common split between sales and other functions. Because Brisley knew that the assessment results would impact many areas outside sales and marketing, he asked executives from other departments to join the customer satisfaction steering committee. This decision, as one Knauf executive said, "was the single best we made in the whole project—and it was a very successful project." The steering committee included decision makers from finance, marketing, manufacturing, logistics, and sales. It is another example of a firm that turned a sales initiative into a business initiative, breaking down internal and external barriers as it did so.

Knauf mailed the in-depth survey to its distributors and received a phenomenal 90+ percent response rate. It showed that Knauf had an excellent relationship with its distributors and also prioritized those areas that needed to be improved. When the survey had been both qualitatively and quantitatively analyzed, the conclusions were presented to the Knauf executive team. Knauf then returned to the video focus groups and had two 20-minute edits made—one targeted at plants that produce residential products and one targeted at plants that manufacture industrial/commercial products. Knauf then sent joint teams of marketing and manufacturing people to each plant (to show both areas supported the study). The Knauf presentation teams gave the overall conclusions and then showed the appropriate video focus group to each of the four shifts (three shifts and a swing shift). An open discussion followed. Knauf paid all employees for their time, another signal of how serious the firm was.

We have again and again seen employees . . . more willing to change their behaviors for customers than . . . for their supervisors.

In the last two decades, we have again and again seen employees who are more willing to change their behaviors for customers than they are willing to change behaviors for their supervisors.

Employees want to do the right thing. In many cases, though, their firm has not told them what the right thing is because it lacked objective customer information. In the absence of that information, employees will simply do whatever they are rewarded for—which may directly contradict what the customer wants. Or, just as common, the right thing in sales is substantially different from the right thing in operations or manufacturing or billing, etc. Knauf creatively used a traditional market research technique that allowed customers to speak directly to its employees, telling them what was right and what was wrong.

Knauf then challenged all employees to do the right things more effectively.

To help its customers and employees, Knauf set up cross-functional multilevel SWAT teams to attack the problems the assessment had isolated. Some of these problems could be fixed quickly; others required 12 months or more. The critical point is that, at a time when Knauf was stretched thin (needing a new plant to meet increased customer demand), employees dived in and fixed the issues the distributors had identified. And the fixes were not temporary. When Knauf repeated its assessment in 2000, there were almost no overlaps between problems uncovered in 2000 and those discovered in the early 1990s. And of the few overlaps identified, the gaps between what the distributors expected and Knauf's performance were significantly smaller than those found in 1993.

The assessment/alignment process was so successful that Knauf considered it important to develop a mission, vision, and values statement that reflected what the company was and what it wanted to be. In the mid-1990s, Knauf developed the following mission, vision, and values statements:

F I G U R E   3–5

Knauf Quality Quest

What are we here to do? (Mission)

To manufacture and market fiberglass insulation products that customers prefer.

What do we want to be? (Vision)

The best national manufacturers of fiberglass insulation products as measured by product quality, service quality, and financial performance.

What are the rules? (Values)

To accomplish our vision, we must . . .

Create an atmosphere of continuous improvement;

Create an attitude of customer satisfaction from the inside out;

Create a sense of dignity in all positions; and

Operate under the priorities of safety, quality, and productivity.

Knauf then carved those statements down to specific objectives and performance goals for employees who interact with the distributors. Through politically savvy project management, the active buy-in of multiple executives and their departments, the direct voice of the customer, and what it admits was more than a little luck, Knauf created a mission, vision, and values statement and developed better internal and better customer relationships. By communicating deeply within the firm, Knauf moved many employees from compliance to customer commitment. And an unintended result of the assessments and SWAT teams was that Knauf's employee satisfaction rose dramatically.

Yet another way to align your organization comes from a firm known for its global customer focus—Marriott International. Marriott is famous for hiring for and continually reinforcing customer focus in its culture—even with the traditionally high turnover of its industry. Marriott's alliance account directors are able to leverage that customer focus with employees around the world by creating global and national teams dedicated to those customers. What makes the case special is that team members receive no direct compensation for serving these accounts—and the results are outstanding.

MARRIOTT INTERNATIONAL'S ALLIANCE ACCOUNT DIRECTORS AND THEIR "VOLUNTEER ARMY"

Marriott International is a global corporation, with 13 brands of hotels and 2,400 total properties in 70 countries. Marriott's global customers are Fortune 100 firms that only want to speak to one Marriott representative. This customer expectation drove the creation of Marriott's Alliance Account program in 1997. The Alliance Account program, with 12 account directors, is now responsible for a portfolio of 30+ accounts that generate more than $800 million of Marriott's total annual business. While alliance account directors are critical, though, they comprise only one half of Marriott's marketing equation.

Marriott employees around the world comprise the other half. When alliance account directors devise a business solution for a global account, they depend on Marriott resources to help implement it. These resources might be national or regional sales leaders, subject-matter experts in information technology (IT), revenue management, operations, telecommunications, finance, or even furniture rental.

While creating the Alliance Account program, Marriott faced the question many organizations face: How can we coordinate the activities of hundreds of employees around the world to ensure that any value-added implementation is transparent to the customer? More critically, how do we get them to devote their time to something for which they will receive no direct compensation?

Steve Richard, VP for alliance accounts, says global cross-functional teams offer an ongoing challenge at Marriott, but the firm has successfully leveraged Marriott's many competencies to serve alliance accounts. An alliance account director will start working with a given customer. She will immerse herself in the account's business challenges and then will start thinking about offering a business solution. She will determine what sort of resources she needs and will request that appropriate Marriott people—anywhere from 5 to 50—meet, sometimes in person, sometimes on the phone. At the meeting she presents the solution she's created, provides the value propositions for both Marriott and the account, and asks for the group's suggestions and assistance.

Richard says that the alliance account director is the team leader, responsible for generating excitement and creating a sense of urgency—what we sometimes call a "burning platform"—for all team members. In most cases, Richard says, employees will do what they can to help. And while they do not receive direct compensation, by implementing the solution, they make the Marriott organization stronger and more nimble and, in many cases, generate more business for their region, market, and/or area of expertise.

Iris Riemann, based in Frankfurt, Germany, a Marriott International alliance account director since 1999, is a perfect example. She serves two global accounts, one of which is Siemens, the $75-billion-dollar electrical engineering and electronics firm. Siemens is based in Munich but has a presence in 190 countries; it has 250,000 travelers a year, almost half based in Germany. These facts create interesting challenges for a global account manager.

Before 1998, when Marriott named Siemens an alliance account, the two firms' relationship was very fragmented, very local—almost nonexistent. In 1997, Siemens took the first step in centralizing its travel management, creating its Corporate Mobility Services (CMS). At the same time, though, Siemens maintained its country travel groups. These groups, each with differing cultural, country, and performance-management standards, report to the Siemens country headquarters, with only a dotted-line relationship to Siemens CMS. So even if Siemens corporate agreed to a special travel arrangement, the country travel groups did not have to comply with that agreement.

When Riemann was named Marriott alliance account director for Siemens, she immediately immersed herself in Siemens' business challenges. In 1998 Marriott had offered Siemens CMS centralized pricing for 1999. When Riemann took over the same year, she pulled together a cross-functional Marriott account team to support the German Siemens travel managers and meeting planners it could locate. Later that year Riemann met with the Siemens' country travel groups, presenting how she and Marriott might help support their travel policies and lower their travel and lodging costs. As she helped the various country groups, Riemann began to act as a link between those travel teams and Siemens' CMS. She found herself providing both groups with information and resources they lacked. All of Siemens travel groups, for example, were glad to receive regular reports listing spend/room night figures for all their travelers.

Centralized pricing and the dedicated Marriott account team worked so well that in late 1999 Riemann and her team extended the relationship with Siemens travel managers in other countries. Riemann contacted Siemens' travel management in the United States, in the United Kingdom, and also in Hong Kong, Singapore and Beijing, all major Siemens markets. Riemann also appointed Marriott account team leaders in these locations to build up local Siemens account teams. Local account teams included alliance account members, market sales leaders, sales leaders of key Marriott hotels, and various subject matter experts. Overall and local team membership changes as Siemens' business challenges change. The most critical addition to the Siemens team was Karl Kilburg, senior vice president for Marriott in Continental Europe, who accepted the role as the Marriott Focused Executive to Siemens globally. Kilburg helped Marriott escalate the relationship to a strategic level, sponsoring a multimillion-dollar joint technical venture between Marriott and Siemens.

Marriott also invited Siemens travel managers to Marriott International headquarters in Washington, D.C., where they met with members of the Siemens account teams, Marriott HQ subject-matter experts, and senior executives representing sales, marketing, and other areas critical to the account. These travel managers appreciated both the ease of doing business with Marriott and Marriott's ability to support their e-business approach within travel management. Riemann and Marriott had set up electronically bookable room allocations through Siemens' TravelNet. Riemann and her team—now numbering between 20 and 30—actively support Siemens Travel Management by increasing use and acceptance of TravelNet. Dedicated Siemens room allocations currently apply only to 15 German hotels, but Marriott will soon roll it out in other European countries where Siemens uses TravelNet.

Since early 2001, Riemann and her team have been adding individual team members in those countries where Marriott has only a few hotels (Poland, Denmark, Canada, etc.). With these teams in place, and with Marriott's ability to support a Global Account Program, Marriott has become Siemens' Corporate Travel Management's "favorite hotel supplier," and is now (since 2001) Siemens' No. 1 hotel company in lodging expenditures.

What has Siemens received from the relationship? Marriott International tracks its alliance accounts average spend/room night. In 2000–2001, the average Siemens traveler spend/room night decreased by $8 from the previous year. (With about 220,000 Siemens room nights per year, total savings comes to $1.76 million per year.) And the Marriott-Siemens high-tech joint venture, bent on bringing the latest web technology to the business traveler, may offer the greatest benefit of all. It is an offering Siemens and Marriott can both use and sell to other hotels.

What value has Marriott received? In 1998, Siemens' listed only 52 Marriott hotels in its preferred hotel directory. In 2000 that number had jumped to 204. In 1998 Marriott sold 100,000 room nights to Siemens. In 2000 that number surged by 80 percent, to 180,000. Since Marriott started treating Siemens as an alliance account, Siemens' annual business with Marriott has gone from $7+ million/year in 1998 to about $17+ million/year in 2001, more than a 140 percent increase.

Reimann is clear that this sales leap would have been impossible without the coordinated and dedicated efforts of Marriott Siemens account teams around the world. Reimann created the initial value propositions and sense of urgency for serving Siemens. She then worked with the teams to refine and deliver those propositions. She managed the communication with and coordination of her account team members.

> The most successful account management programs are based on data—financial and customer-based—and are committed to continuous improvement.

She calls these team members her "volunteer army" and it is an apt phrase—even though the vast majority of team members do not report to her. Marriott has continually shown itself able to align around the needs of its largest accounts—a rare and, as we have seen, a very profitable skill.

Marriott has successfully made its Alliance Account program a business initiative for critical customers and broken down divisional barriers, just as Knauf, Minnesota Power, and

Honeywell did. Firms that successfully implement strategic account management usually need to align internal relationships and processes before, during, and after the program's launch. In our experience, the most successful account management programs are based on data—financial and customer-based—and are committed to continuous improvement.

CREATE FIRM ALIGNMENT

What can you do to ensure that your firm is aligned for strategic account management?

1. Make certain you have:
   - Clear corporate and account management strategies on which to align;
   - Clear value statements to guide the alignment; and
   - Internal communication programs that drive and reinforce those visions deeply into the organization.
2. Develop a "voice of the customer" program to help employees walk in the customers' shoes.
3. Conduct regular and multiple types of assessments on critical customer relationships.
4. Drive robust customer information deep into the organization. At one point, Disney was supposed to have more than 200 ways of listening to its customers. How many ways does your firm listen to critical accounts?
5. Customize cross-functional teams to solve account problems as they arise.

CHAPTER 4

Key 3: Start with the Right Number of the Right Strategic Accounts

Strategic account management is as much about deselecting accounts you don't want as it is about selecting the accounts you do.

Das Narayandas, Ph.D., Harvard Business School[1]

In this chapter we will discuss the need for focusing on the right number of the right kind of strategic accounts. We'll discuss:

1. How to examine strategic accounts.
2. How to conduct a high-level portfolio analysis.
3. Using strategic account selection criteria.

Firms moving into strategic account management are sometimes tempted to start big—either by starting their program with 150 strategic accounts or by simply declaring their 50 largest revenue producers strategic accounts (whether or not they are profitable). Potential problems are bound to arise if a supplier chooses either direction and aggressively pro-

---

[1] Written in a note to the authors in April 2000.

motes—before rollout—the program's heightened service and relationship quality. If a company makes pre-rollout promises, suppliers, in our experience, will almost certainly find huge broken or nonexistent processes and systems early in their account management implementation. These processes may require months or even years to fix, and, while they are being fixed, customers will not receive their promised service levels.

The danger in choosing customers solely for their revenue levels is that you may find yourself making large investments for little or negative return. We have seldom conducted a portfolio analysis in which there wasn't some huge revenue producer that was unprofitable. There may be a reason to keep such an account: it may be a marquee account, a slowly emerging opportunity, or an overhead account. But in our experience, if a firm has enough overhead accounts, its balance sheet can start repelling investors. The unexamined customer, in our experience, is often not worth having.

The unexamined customer, in our experience, is often not worth having.

WAYS TO EXAMINE STRATEGIC ACCOUNTS

What is a strategic account? Strategic accounts are customers who most readily help a firm achieve its strategic and financial goals. As one firm's chief sales officer said in responding to this definition, "I get it. The problem I'm having is that we don't have a real sales strategy except for hitting our numbers every month." Suppliers without strategies often simply declare large revenue producers and/or marquee customers strategic and, in many cases, they remain so forever. Other firms have developed different strategies for each of a small number of accounts, which is less cost-efficient than an overall marketing strategy, but at least this is better than ad hoc strategic account management (as Honeywell IACS discovered).

Firms with clear strategies often enjoy another distinction with strategic accounts: as the relationship progresses, it changes. Accounts begin to see your firm not as a vendor de-

FIGURE 4-1

The Buy-Sell Hierarchy

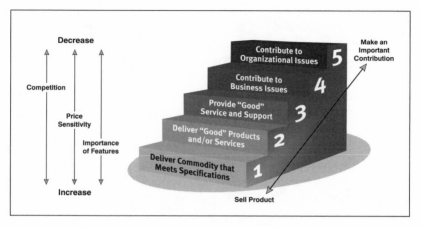

livering a commodity, but perhaps as a chosen supplier delivering differentiated value—through various kinds of contributions. A handy tool can help you both classify how your accounts see the value you provide and help you determine how to move those accounts to the next level. We call this tool the Buy-Sell Hierarchy.[2] Understanding where your customers perceive you to be on the Buy-Sell Hierarchy is important when determining the resources and costs required to grow customer relationships.

At the lowest level of the buy-sell hierarchy, the account sees you as a commodity vendor, competing purely on price. At this level you will need to continue price competition unless you can move up the buy-sell hierarchy. If you move up the steps, the account may then recognize you as differentiating on product (level 2) or service quality (level 3). Given the emphasis on product and service quality in the last 20 years, in many markets quality is the price of entry. If product and service quality offer a way to differentiate, in many cases, the differentiation is short-lived. If your strategic account manager, however, can truly start helping your accounts with business and organiza-

---

[2] ©Miller Heiman, Inc.

tional issues (levels 4 and 5)—helping their revenues grow, minimizing their costs, positioning them more effectively in the marketplace—the relationship can change dramatically. Few suppliers make it to these top two levels. But those who do find their accounts treat them as "trusted advisors,"[3] in the words of David H. Maister, combining high levels of technical expertise and interpersonal skills to help their customers. As difficult as these levels are to achieve, at this level of relationship, competition is almost nonexistent and value flows freely in both directions.

But some customers would never allow this business/organization level of relationship. They tend to see suppliers as vendors, period. If one of your strategic accounts does not see the value in your increased investments, or thanks you for them and asks for deep discounts, it may make little sense to keep defining them as strategic or to invest more in the relationship. It is a very hard lesson for some firms, but some clients just want a good product at a good price—nothing more. We have seen customers tell suppliers to get rid of the extra services—such as a strategic account manager—and to remove those service costs from the prices they are paying.

As one example of buyers who prefer straight vendors, a high-tech manufacturer in the 1990s named several hundred large revenue producers as "enterprise" customers. Then, before program rollout, the firm conducted a follow-up and wide-ranging portfolio analysis on those accounts. The analysis determined that a significant proportion of these customers was not looking for a strategic supplier, but rather for a vendor. They preferred an inside salesperson to sell them, not a strategic account manager. Whoever suggested the portfolio analysis should have received a huge bonus because it saved the high-tech firm tens of millions of dollars in unwanted sales and service costs. The portfolio analysis also caused the firm to create different sales channels to sell to the customers in the ways they preferred to buy. Before rolling out strategic account management, customer assessments and portfolio analyses are

---

[3] Maister, David H., et al (2000). *The Trusted Advisor*. New York: The Free Press.

more than just good ideas. They can guide your strategic planning tremendously and help you wisely invest your resources.

You also might copy another approach to initiating strategic account management by examining what a medium-sized manufacturer did in the mid-nineties. The firm started its strategic account management pilot by focusing on three of its five largest and most critical customers—its co-destiny accounts. It chose the three after in-depth account assessments and portfolio analyses (which found that the other two accounts had very low profitability at best). There was no question that these three firms deserved a higher level of attention. The supplier's only concern was whether it would receive a clear return on its strategic investment.

The firm therefore started the implementation not with promises, but by letting the three customers know that it would like a closer relationship with each of them. The supplier needed to develop new processes and systems, but by treating each of these as a value-added initiative and presenting them as such, all three accounts were very pleased by the program. The new closeness that developed through the changed systems and processes allowed the SAM to understand the accounts' needs more deeply than she had before. Within 18 months, the supplier was doing joint R&D projects with two customers and working on a large joint venture with the third account. The supplier's strategic initiative had also increased its revenues with these three accounts by almost 50 percent, with significantly increased profitability.

Twenty-four months later, the supplier started rolling out the program to another five large customers. It was more than comfortable with the ROI on its first investment in strategic account management—both in dollars and in greater customer loyalty.

The next year, the supplier created a second pilot for a "junior strategic account management" program, which leveraged the systems and processes already developed to focus on medium-sized customers with large opportunities. The supplier staffed the junior program with people whom it thought had the skills to be strategic account managers. The firm thought of the junior pilot as the account management "farm" system, where people could learn as they developed customers. As it happened, the medium-sized account management program generated millions in incremental revenue and trained 10 account managers who were soon ready for the "big leagues." This two-sided program became the single most effective marketing initiative the firm had launched. The supplier attributed its success to going slowly, starting with an intent rather than with promises, developing processes as needed, and quantifying the value it delivered along the way.

Defining too many customers as strategic too often makes it very difficult for the program to demonstrate a timely return. A firm that sees itself as having been burned might justifiably resist continuing strategic account management. Trying to focus on too many customers is also an excellent way to waste valuable resources, which in turn may force SAMs to focus on generating more short-term revenue—to become, in our definition from Chapter 1, key account sellers. You can better optimize your returns from strategic accounts by aligning around a common vision and strategy, selecting the right people to manage customers, training those account managers, setting up a human-resources support system, and ensuring that the customers you select are best suited for a strategic account approach.

Identifying a "right" account starts with strategic alignment, followed by an account assessment, including a customer portfolio analysis. Because such portfolio analyses can be very complex, with activities-based costing and predicted margins, we have provided below a simpler way to conduct a high-level portfolio analyses.

HOW TO CONDUCT A HIGH-LEVEL PORTFOLIO ANALYSIS: THE SIX-QUESTION MEETING

We first assume that you already have relationships with some accounts you are thinking about making "strategic." Start your analysis by scheduling a meeting—ideally face-to-face—with representatives from various divisions and departments

FIGURE 4-2

Account Portfolio Analysis

	Previous			Future	
	Two Years Ago	Last Year	This Year	Next Year	Year After Next
Add Revenue					
Subtract Direct Cost					
Subtract Indirect Cost					
Equals Net Revenue					

whose people directly interface with your targeted accounts. Focus on no more than two or three customers, depending on the complexity of the relationships. Consider this meeting a pilot for an ongoing value-determination process, which you can usually customize to your firm's particular needs. Send the six questions below in advance to meeting participants. The questions will form the meeting agenda. Answering them can start to give you a reliable handle on which customers are generating—and which customers are bleeding—net revenue.

1. How much total revenue has each location of the targeted strategic accounts generated over the last three years? What is your revenue projection for these locations over the next two years? If you have a sophisticated and centralized financial system, answering this first question may take no more than a few keystrokes. But if your organization and systems are at all decentralized, this can be a particularly valuable exercise.

2. What does it cost annually to serve these customers? Estimate costs for the last three years and the next two.

The regional people should have a good handle on the direct costs of serving these targeted accounts. But traditional accounting tends to allocate its overhead costs into its margin numbers based on sales volume. This means that, if the customer is generating 50 percent of a supplier's revenue, the supplier allocates 50 percent of its overhead costs to that customer. The challenge here is that some of these allocated overhead costs (such as corporate office rent) are not directly related to managing customer relationships. And some costs tend to be excluded from traditional margin calculation—indirect costs such as extraordinary-warranty or customer-service costs. Here we are looking for these special costs—extraordinary handholding, unbudgeted project management, unscheduled line runs, unplanned IT costs—anything that might have slipped by traditional costing in the last three years. Such inclusions and exclusions can dramatically skew true margins. Then estimate costs in dollars to serve those three accounts for the next two years.

This can be a particularly interesting question to address. One supplier told us that this question "told us more about our customers than we really wanted to know." Another, after factoring in an estimated margin percentage, quickly learned that its number-two revenue producer was, in fact, unprofitable (they'd suspected it for years). Other disturbing issues can arise. At one high-tech firm the salespeople were "throwing in" the maintenance contract free to get the sale. That contract, the operations people patiently explained, was the high-tech firm's single most profitable offering. In several cases, to get the order, the salespeople had given away hundreds of thousands of dollars in repeatable future cash flow to the account. No one had explained to them the impact of doing this; they were compensated for revenue, not profit.

When a supplier starts rolling up costs to serve, eyes can widen and previously uncaptured costs quickly multiply. These numbers are still estimates, but in this case, estimates will usually give the supplier a much better handle on which customers/ divisions provide real value and therefore deserve to be served strategically.

3. Subtract estimated costs from estimated revenues for each account to get a margin estimate for the last three and the next two years.

   The estimates here will be enlightening— occasionally shocking—because so few firms have attempted this exercise.

4. What is the growth potential of these accounts? How long would it take to realize that growth?

   Here is where business intelligence can make or save you a great deal of money. If you can identify which customers or which customer divisions offer dramatic growth opportunities, you can select and invest in pilot strategic accounts that offer the greatest potential payback. This cross-functional meeting is an excellent time for people to share the customers' particular challenges or what they see as the accounts' opportunities. Field service people, for example, may know of a customer challenge, but if they are not aware of their firm's total competencies, they may not see that challenge as an opportunity. But if they share what they saw or heard, someone else at the meeting may see it for the opportunity it is. This sort of cross-functional pollenization can also reinforce firm alignment and team building, and can bring revenue generation and profitability top of mind for everyone. Answering this question can also be the first step in developing or refining an account planning process—because in many cases the answers can point out a glaring gap in the supplier's account intelligence.

5. Where are these accounts on the transactional-to-strategic buyer continuum?

   Using 1 as a purely transactional customer and 3 as an account that is looking for a strategic partnership, what numbers would you assign to each of the customers you are currently thinking about serving strategically? Before the cross-functional meeting, ask the attendees to classify the targeted customers' buying orientation. While there may be some differences in customer divisions, we've always been surprised at the level of agreement about which accounts are transaction- and cost-focused and which think in terms of strategic relationships. If you assign many 2s, make a second pass at each customer/division and try to force a choice. Answering these questions can really help determine which customers are worth serving strategically.

There is a tremendous first-mover advantage to determining which customers are truly profitable and which are not.

Several years ago, a manufacturing executive gave a presentation at a small marketing gathering. He said that his firm's goal was to help his competitors go out of business, and to that end his firm was conducting very sophisticated loyalty and profitability analyses on its customer base. He and his firm wanted to determine where true value really lay and, just as important, where it didn't. Once his firm determined which customers were bleeding value, he said those customers were, one way or another, going to be migrated to the competition. He believed those accounts "were customers the competition really deserved." Within 18 months, the program bore fruit: a major competitor that had absorbed many of the manufacturer's cast-off customers had dropped out of the market. There is a tremendous first-mover advantage to determining which customers are truly profitable and which are not.

6. Is there anything else we haven't asked you about these customers that you think we should know?

   This is a catch-all question, but in a number of cases it will bring up something that has not been discussed or an opportunity that you didn't see before. We recommend using it at the end of the meeting when everything is still fresh in the attendees' minds.

We have kept this discussion at a fairly high level. We now have an example of a firm that, using an approach similar to the one we just presented, analyzed its customer portfolio, actually dropped more than 100 customers (from a total of 157) over time, and in the process doubled revenues and tripled margins.

THE GfK CUSTOM RESEARCH INC. STORY: HOW ONE FIRM CUT 66 PERCENT OF ITS CUSTOMERS, DOUBLED ITS REVENUES, TRIPLED ITS MARGINS, AND WON THE BALDRIGE AWARD

Founded in 1974, GfK Custom Research Incorporated (CRI) is a market research firm with offices in Minneapolis, San Francisco, and New York. CRI has 140+ employees, and in 1998 generated $30+ million annually with a highly focused "core" partner management program. The firm's total client base in 1998 consisted of 80 customers, 36 of which CRI considered core partners—CRI's elite customer status. CRI had nine account managers and nine account teams, each of which managed 1 to 5 major customers and whose charge is to help the business grow at these assigned—and very carefully screened—customers.

How CRI screened those customers in 1987 is an excellent example of a firm conducting a portfolio analysis to determine customer value. Wanting to grow from its $10+ million in revenue, CRI took a serious look at its 157 customers to decide where its true financial opportunities lay. CRI classified its customers' value into four "quadrants," which CRI co-owner and partner, Jeff Pope, describes:

FIGURE 4–3

Customer Value Clarifications

High Volume Low Margin	High Volume High Margin
Low Volume Low Margin	Low Volume High Margin

I. High Volume & Low Margin. About half of these customers were new ones that CRI figured would become more profitable. The other half were on the verge of the high-volume, high-profit quadrant.

II. High Volume & High Margin. These customers had a supplier reduction program and valued an ongoing relationship with CRI. There were only 10 of these customers, but they accounted for roughly 30 percent of sales.

III. Low Volume & Low Margin. CRI once believed it could make many of these customers more loyal, but time revealed that this group wanted to work with numerous research firms.

IV. Low Volume & High Margin. These were small customers who were very profitable, but the key issue for assigned account managers was whether there was more potential for sales.

In 1988, after using activities-based costing and internal meetings to classify its customers on these quadrants, CRI realized that only 10 clients fell into the most desirable quadrant (High/High). The firm also discovered that 100+ customers provided very little, if anything, to CRI's top or bottom line. When CRI factored in selling and administrative costs, such as ongoing proposal writing, many of these customers were value "bleeders." CRI owners and partners realized that they had been paying so much attention to its top 30 customers—by revenue—that they had never really prioritized their total customer base, some of whom were Fortune 1000 firms, albeit unprofitable.

We often ask executives if their firm would benefit from removing 5 percent of its lowest-performing customer relationships. They usually reply that there would be large benefits: allocating sales resources to higher-value customers, getting rid of a customer group that tends to have too many service requests relative to their generated revenue, and potentially getting rid of several support people who spend most of their time with these smaller customers. Many firms suspect or know that they are serving unprofitable customers, but very few analyze their customers on a case-by-case basis, looking at the each customer's revenue, direct costs, selling costs, and true profit. And of those firms that have conducted that sort of portfolio analysis, even fewer have done what CRI then did—during the next few years they let the marginal customers go so they could concentrate on the "core" partners. In other words, they began to manage their customers as a portfolio of relationship assets.

This was not a simple or easy process—removing customers is as counterintuitive a move as a sales-based firm can make.

But CRI let those clients go (most by not responding to RFPs) and concentrated on its high-value account relationships. By 1992, the results were already evident: CRI's sales had grown to $16 million—a 45 percent leap over 1987's numbers.

To continue the positive growth, CRI systematized the quadrants' lessons by setting up account-selection criteria or gates through which a prospective customer must pass before it is accepted as a strategic account. The selection process, initiated in 1988, has been substantially refined. It begins when a prospective client or customer calls in with a potential job. The company routes that prospect to CRI professionals, some of whom have 20 years of experience. In the course of the conversation, these professionals ask a series of questions to determine if the job and the customer are true opportunities. While Beth Rounds, senior VP at CRI, emphasized that this screening is *not* an interrogation, she said CRI does ask these six questions:

1. How did you hear about us? The best answer here is that the caller received a referral from a firm that CRI had helped (90 percent of CRI's business is from referrals). If someone is calling in simply because they saw the firm's name somewhere (an Internet or industry directory, for example), the call may be purely transactional, which other questions will reveal.

2. What kind of work is it (in terms of industry or scope)? The answer here allows CRI gatekeepers to identify whether the caller's request is outside CRI's expertise, in which case CRI recommends indirect competitors. This question also allows the gatekeepers to tell whether the caller is simply price shopping.

3. What's your budget? This may seem to justify a "none-of-your-business" response, but the gatekeepers have the experience to make a ballpark estimate based on the answer to question #2. They can then see if there are major gaps between the job and the budget, in which case the job is turned down.

4. What are your decision criteria? CRI turns thumbs down on any blind bidding or decision-by-committee situations. They know that bidding wars and long, drawn-out committee decisions can dramatically erode margins.

5. Who are we competing against for your business? Given the type of job, CRI knows who their true value-based competitors are. When gatekeepers hear those names, they know the caller has done some research to find the best. If the caller names three price-based competitors, CRI knows it would be better off handing the business to those competitors.

6. What's the reason behind your call? If the prospective client has a legitimate need for a new supplier (if a past supplier has stopped providing value, for example), CRI will look at it closely. But if CRI senses the caller is doing some end-of-the-year price shopping, the potential job can die here.

Rounds estimates that fewer than 10 percent of the approximately 25 incoming calls per month make it through these questions. Rounds, however, has several cautions for firms wanting to copy CRI's screening questions. First, the questions are not foolproof. It is still possible to get "a great interviewee," someone who says all the right things but can't do what he says. He may, for example, lack the budget or the power. The second caution is that there are times when an answer that normally would be considered "wrong" is overlooked if there is a strategic reason for doing so—if, for example, the job represents a major inroad into a particularly desirable client. But the questions allow CRI to be selective about whom they want as customers.

CRI can quantify virtually all the benefits of its approach. In 1988, CRI had 157 customers and $10+ million in revenues. By 1998, it had cut its customer base to 80 (some of which were Fortune 100 firms). Its revenues had tripled to $30 million, and its margins had doubled. In 1996, CRI also won the Malcolm Baldrige National Quality Award, at that time the smallest service firm ever to do so. There are serious opportunities for bottom-line improvement by serving the right strategic accounts.

USING STRATEGIC ACCOUNT SELECTION CRITERIA

This section provides additional ways to select the "right" customers and a list of strategic account selection criteria. We will also show how these criteria can be used to create an interim marketing strategy.

Over the years we have seen a wide range of strategic account selection criteria. Three teams at one client came up with more than 150 selection criteria, some of which are shown in Figure 4–4.

Many businesspeople find it difficult to move beyond revenue and profitability selection criteria. If your program's major goals are solely financial, however, you may be focusing on key account selling rather than strategic account management. Strategic account management requires a delicate balance. Your program has to generate the bottom-line return to justify its existence, but at the same time you have to re-envision the future continually to optimize as-yet-unseen strategic opportunities. In Frederick Reichheld's *The Loyalty Effect*, Dave Illingworth, group-VP of Lexus North America, makes this point very effectively: "The more you focus on the bottom line, the harder it is to hit."[4] Illingworth is presenting Toyota's approach to the market, which focuses on the elements that drive customer loyalty. By doing so, Toyota generated an amazing financial success story.

Another pitfall to watch for when generating selection criteria is that choosing eight or nine of them is really too many for the firm to remember, let alone act on. The best customer management firms tend to work with three to five account selection criteria, all of which ideally come from their strategy. In other words, those criteria answer the question: "Given our firm's

---

[4]   Reichheld, Frederick F. (1996). *The Loyalty Effect:The Hidden Force Behind Growth, Profits, and Lasting Value.* (p.168). Boston: Harvard University Press.

F I G U R E 4–4

Representative Strategic Account Selection Criteria

1. Revenue potential.
2. Profitability potential.
3. Marquee value.
4. Centralized purchasing.
5. Many opportunities at many locations.
6. Market leader.
7. Effect on major competitors of gaining this customer.
8. Existing executive relationships.
9. Complementary technologies.
10. Reputation for loyalty to suppliers.
11. Rigorous supplier certification program.
12. Buying orientation (strategic vs. transactional).
13. Cultural "fit" between companies.
14. Compatible or complementary systems.
15. Company's solvency.
16. Quick pay.
17. Can leverage us into a new technology.
18. Can leverage us into a new region, country, continent.
19. Product fit.
20. Flexibility.
21. Common raw materials base.
22. Acceptable acquisition cost (workable decision group).
23. They have existing strategic supplier alliances.
24. Innovative, state-of-the-art practices (R&D, manufacturing, etc.).
25. Potential customer has a value-added marketing strategy.
26. Potential customer has shown a repeated willingness to outsource.
27. Potential process synergy.
28. Expertise in competencies we need (inventory management, logistics, etc.).
29. Honest in its dealings.
30. Can be a channel partner for our offering.

marketing strategy, why are we focusing on these accounts?" By closely tying strategy and selection criteria, suppliers reinforce their firm's alignment and focus. And in so doing, these firms tend to succeed.

Firms lacking a clear customer management strategy can also list five or so selection criteria—revenue, profitability, and three other criteria—and then work backward to develop an interim marketing strategy, to be refined as needed. This can work very well if an executive cross-functional group develops and implements the selection criteria. The key point is that, ideally, the strategy and selection criteria complement each other. Otherwise, the firm's direction will not be as clear as it needs to be for alignment. And its returns will not be as significant.

START WITH THE RIGHT NUMBER OF THE RIGHT STRATEGIC ACCOUNTS

How Can You Ensure That Your Firm Is Selecting the Right Number of the Right Kind of Strategic Accounts?

1. Conduct a high-level portfolio analysis of a few targeted existing customers to determine which create and which bleed value. Have a cross-functional meeting to get answers to the six questions in this chapter.
2. Let this high-level portfolio analysis become the beginning of an ongoing process for determining lifetime account value.
3. Be clear about your firm's overall strategy and tie your strategic account selection criteria back to that strategy.
4. Start strategic account management with a pilot, focusing on two or three of your most critical accounts.
5. Slowly expand your program to include other customers. Be humble: promise nothing you cannot deliver.

Tactical Issues in Strategic Account Management . . . Ironbolt Steel and Executive Visits: What Didn't Work

Jonas Simon, president of Ironbolt Steel, had spent the last 15 months aligning his organization, hiring strategic account managers, and sending them out to develop better relationships with his largest customers. He knew that it had been time well spent, but he was not really a patient man. It went against his grain to go so long without being able just to tell someone to do something in strategic accounts. And then he had what he felt was a moment of brilliance. For years, he had personally visited each of these large accounts (he had started in field sales and loved the contact). Simon had been so successful with these visits that Ironbolt now had too many customers and Jonas too little time to visit each personally. This fact created an opportunity for Jonas to act.

Jonas decided that strategic account visits offered a wonderful opportunity to ensure that his executives remained "engaged marketers." He also believed that *all* his executives would benefit from such visits. So at a quarterly executive meeting, he announced that every executive would make six customer calls—by themselves—every year. He gave out the names of six customers and the contacts that each executive would visit. To him the entire assignment was a no-brainer.

Thus executive visits began. From his salespeople, his customer service people, his strategic account managers, and from the customers themselves, he started hearing horror stories.

Jonas' vice president of MIS had visited one of Ironbolt's top-five customers. After hearing the customer's president criticize "his" EDI system for being slow and hard to use, the VP of MIS calmly replied that the president lacked the technical skills to even understand his system, let alone criticize it.

Ironbolt's CFO was very uncomfortable about visiting customers. He got together long financial printouts so he would have something to talk about. He ended up giving a 90-minute in-depth,100-slide financial presentation to another executive at a top-five customer. The customer executive called Jonas and said—in emphatic tones—that he would up his purchases with Ironbolt if Jonas would guarantee that he would never have to sit through another of those presentations. Jonas momentarily considered using the CFO as part of a very creative sales and marketing strategy. He quickly realized, however, that the CFO marketing approach was impossible.

Jonas' VP of human resources believed that she could best develop trust with her assigned customer by sharing Ironbolt information. She enthusiastically and repeatedly emphasized what a great financial year Ironbolt was having and how such resources made Ironbolt a truly stable supplier. After her visit, the customer executive called Jonas and said that, if Ironbolt was having such a great year financially, why couldn't Jonas give him a deeper discount on rolled steel?

Jonas felt an executive migraine coming on.

✦✦✦

Jonas had gone through the hard work to get all his employees headed in roughly the same direction, had selected targeted strategic accounts, and had carefully assigned his strategic account managers. But his well-intentioned executive visit program had some unintended consequences.

It was not enough for Jonas—or any other firm—to do the strategic alignment work and then assume he could do something to help strategic accounts without asking basic questions and setting up support structures both for his executives and for his strategic account management program. Jonas needed to ask his SAMs how to integrate his executive visit program into the goals of their strategic account plans. He also needed to ask whether all of his executives were really equipped to speak to customers (a firm usually has a few decision makers who probably should never speak to customers). And he needed to help determine presentations that would offer the customers value without giving away the store.

After the strategic alignment work, there are tactical issues you ignore at your peril, among which are: creating human-resource support for your account management program (Chapter 5); developing firmwide relationships (Chapter 6), which require far more direction than Jonas' approach above; quantifying value received from and delivered to strategic accounts (Chapter 7); and using technology in strategic account management (Chapter 8).

Key 4: Create Human Resources Support for Strategic Account Managers

If I could implement (national account management) again, I'd insist on having more of the infrastructure in place before we went to market.

Tom VanHootegem
Director National Accounts
Boise Office Solutions[1]

Throughout this book, we talk about different support structures required by strategic account management. Excellent firms/programs tend to see their account managers as human assets, fundamental to their success. This chapter will concentrate on four of the most critical of these human-resource support issues:

1. How do we select strategic account managers?
2. How do we develop strategic account managers?
3. How do we assign strategic account managers?
4. How do we pay strategic account managers?

---

[1] From an interview the authors conducted with Tom VanHootegem in May 2001.

As we have seen, some firms confuse key account selling with strategic account management, and assume that a good frontline salesperson will make a good strategic account manager. They therefore just look for their most productive salespeople. Because these salespeople already know how to sell, their firms may see little need for developing them into SAMs. And because the old method of assigning customers and compensation always worked with these salespeople, their organizations often see little reason to change these, either.

Suppliers, by not knowing the expectations of all the buying influences in the account's decision-making group, have woven the noose that hung them.

While the key account selling approach works well in generating short-term revenue, it can easily lead to relationship problems, should a customer expect a truly strategic relationship. In too many cases, suppliers, by not knowing the expectations of all the buying influences in the account's decision-making group, have woven the noose that hung them.

They have created a human-resource infrastructure that usually overassigns the key account sellers and rewards them for focusing primarily on quarter-to-quarter revenue, paying them well to meet only a few of the account's expectations.

The key account seller approach, which often generates significant revenue, leaves the door wide open to a competitive supplier offering a true strategic relationship. An example: we know of a high-tech supplier that in the mid 1990s provided its key account sellers little training, assigned them 40+ accounts each, and based their compensation heavily on commissions. One of this firm's largest—and oldest—customers was a services firm that generated $300,000+ a year in business. After 10 years, the services firm suddenly dropped the high-tech supplier from its approved vendor list. When we spoke to the SAM who later recovered the account (after almost 3 years), he told us that his firm had lost that customer's business because the high-tech supplier had been complacent in both its service levels and presentation of value. Instead of searching continuously for new value propositions, the supplier responded only to account requests.

But those were not the only problems.

The key account seller who had lost the account used to sell—or, rather, took orders from—one person in procurement. Trying to cover his 40+ accounts, he had neither the time nor inclination to analyze the services firm's decision-making units or its purchasing practices. He did not bother to see if his firm was offering the appropriate internal people an ongoing, competitive, and compelling value equation. He had not developed metrics to measure his firm's performance at the services firm. In managing the services firm, neither the key account seller nor the high-tech supplier really understood what was at stake. This remained the case until the services firm's newly hired VP of procurement analyzed all his firm's supplier relationships. When he audited the high-tech supplier's relationship with his firm, he saw little value and kicked them out.

The key account seller did exactly what he was asked to do—continue to generate revenue from many accounts. And so he skimmed relationships to generate the cash. The service firm's VP of procurement, however, expected suppliers to develop more internal relationships, to measure their performance, and to regularly quantify their value delivered. In other words, the high-tech supplier was sending a tactician— and a good one—to manage a customer where a critical—and unknown—person wanted a more strategic relationship. The high-tech supplier had created a human-resource infrastructure that paid the key account seller well to do the wrong things for this customer—to think and sell short-term. Quarter-to-quarter revenue generation is, of course, a critical way to measure a strategic account manager's success; but just as critical is truly understanding what the customer expects, how it buys, what its business challenges are. Answering those questions can allow the revenue stream to grow exponentially.

When the new strategic account manager recovered the service firm's business after three years, the firm initially generated tens of thousands of dollars a year in business. After an additional nine months, though, the account manager had developed the former $300,000-a-year customer into more than a $2 million-a-year account. The supplier, which hired the new account manager for his strategic acumen, assigned him the one account, and compensated him mostly by salary, with some incentive bonuses tied to account share and profitability. The high-tech supplier's payback for making this investment was huge—huge enough for it to rethink how it was selling to certain customers. The high-tech supplier asked the account manager who had recovered the services firm relationship to help the firm develop what they now saw as true strategic account management.

The four steps the high-tech strategic account manager took with the services firm included: (1) conducting an in-depth situation appraisal, (2) developing a strategy for winning the business back, (3) implementing his action plan, and (4) looking ahead/developing another strategy for expanding the business. At a high level, this is the repeatable sales process that every successful strategic account manager takes to secure business and relationships.[2]

We have been discussing possible pitfalls when decision makers don't ask the right questions about human-resource support issues. Let's return to this chapter's initial questions and see how to approach human-resources support more systematically and effectively.

HOW DO WE SELECT STRATEGIC ACCOUNT MANAGERS?

Once a firm decides to move to strategic account management, it needs to locate people who have both patience and strategic acumen. How do we find people who can, in two and a half

---

[2] The best in-depth look at this process comes in Miller, R.B. & Heiman, S.E. (1992). *Successful Large Account Management*. New York: Warner Books.

years, recover and then build a lost customer from nothing to a $2 million-a-year account?

Sophisticated suppliers now are using fairly new competency models to select and develop SAMs. Ten years ago, competency models for SAMs did not really exist—although the Fortune 100 firms were using many kinds of sales-competency models. In the late 1990s, H. R. Chally, a sales-research and -selection firm in Kettering, Ohio, developed one competency model for SAMs.

Chally went to Boise Office Solutions, Lennox Industries, Marriott, Occidental Chemical, Pitney-Bowes of Canada, Reynolds & Reynolds, the Trane Companies, and a number of other firms to ask them for access to excellent strategic account managers and those whose performance was only so-so. Chally conducted in-depth assessments of the account managers to determine the skills that the excellent SAMs displayed, as well as the skills shown by the not-so-excellent account managers. Chally then developed a strategic account manager competency model and employment skills testing, which provides *predictive* accuracy that goes well beyond typical standardized, psychological, personality, skill, competency, or assessment-center tests. Their model appears below.

THE H. R. CHALLY STRATEGIC ACCOUNT MANAGER COMPETENCY MODEL[3]

H. R. Chally's strategic account manager competency model revolves around these five skill areas: the ability and willingness to

1. Take initiative.
2. Commit time and effort to ensure success.
3. Provide proactive assistance/support.
4. Develop technical competencies.
5. Train others.

---

[3] Used with permission from John Wood at H. R. Chally, Kettering, Ohio.

F I G U R E   5–1

The H. R. Chally Strategic Account Manager
Competency Model

Takes Initiative	High Scores	Low Scores
• Positions self as a champion. • Initiates plans and suggestions for reaching goals. • Self-sufficient and sees tasks and responsibilities through to completion.	• Positions self as a champion and will push to set plans and reach goals. • Likes to take charge. • Will follow up and see tasks through to completion.	• Hesitant to push own ideas or drive new goals or plans. • Tends to procrastinate or wait for orders rather than proactively follow up.

In Figure 5–1 we define the skill areas, as well as how strong and weak performers tend to score in the assessment.

At its strongest, taking initiative tends to be associated with risk taking. Most often the skill is manifested by individuals who notice a gap or problem in the organization and take it upon themselves to find and implement a solution. Such people, when they are trying to overcome barriers to productivity, are comfortable with "begging forgiveness rather than asking permission."

Those with higher scores actively manage their plans and stay alert to potential obstacles. They have alternatives ready when things don't go as originally planned, so problems don't jeopardize the overall outcome (Figure 5–2).

This scale originally used a sample of consultative salespeople who tended to achieve higher results in direct proportion to the time they were willing to commit. People who demonstrate this skill thrive on working and place a high value not only on accomplishing the tasks specified in their job description, but devoting the additional time necessary for planning, preparation, and skill development.

High-scoring individuals typically use the extra time to develop more in-depth plans to achieve their objectives. They also build personal sales tools and tracking processes to

F I G U R E   5–2

Chally on Time and Effort

Commits Time and Effort to Ensure Success	High Scores	Low Scores
• Sets job as a first priority. • Willingness to work long hours to meet objectives but does not simply clock hours. • Self-developmental. • Prepares plan to ensure success.	• Invests time according to the goals that must be met. • Values success and money, and "lives to work." • Takes personal responsibility for own life and success. • Open to constructive criticism and driven toward self-improvement. • Prefers to be in control by achieving goals and preparing action steps regularly.	• More inclined to work by the clock than to commit resources as required by the objective. • "Works to live" and does not make career a high priority. • Lacks concern for feedback and motivation to improve skills. • Doesn't see opportunities to control success by preparing special actions.

increase their sales volume and margins. They tend to believe that the basic job is accomplished between 9 and 5, and the effort required to be a top performer is spent from 5 to 9 (Figure 5–3).

This skill is derived from a motivational scale, and as a result, a variety of behaviors can provide the desired satisfaction. Typically, those with a strong need to provide proactive assistance derive a genuine satisfaction from giving advice and helping others to learn and grow. They take responsibility for motivating others to learn the important things that will contribute to their long-term success. They will gladly deal with the very basic or rudimentary issues to bring a novice up to speed because they enjoy seeing the light bulb go on.

Those who provide proactive assistance also derive satisfaction from being appreciated, having the opportunity to demonstrate their expertise and wisdom and being seen as

FIGURE 5-3

Chally on Proactive Assistance

Provides Proactive Assistance and Support	High Scores	Low Scores
• Gains personal satisfaction from volunteering assistance or advice to others. • Patient with individuals in a learning mode and seeks methods for sustaining their motivation and enthusiasm to learn. • Takes personal pride in the success of learners. • Enjoys being held in high esteem by individuals being helped.	• Enjoys teaching and developing others. • Motivated by the opportunity to be seen by others as a mentor and takes pride in others' success. • Takes the initiative to give advice or assistance.	• Does not like to volunteer unsolicited advice. • Impatient with individuals who lack the motivation or enthusiasm to learn what is being taught.

mentors or models. Lastly, seeing learners blossom and demonstrate new-found skill creates a great sense of pride and shared triumph (Figure 5–4).

In all businesses, some functions are more critical to success than others. Depending upon the nature and driving forces of the business, critical functions could be in engineering, marketing, finance, or production.

Strategic account managers who succeed in those businesses must learn the basic technical information and understand the core technologies. Even if their background is in a different area, individuals who score high typically are intellectually curious and enjoy learning. For example, in the business world, someone who has technical competence in the engineering world may need to learn finance to understand the cost analysis associated with certain technical or engineering applications. There is a natural quest to stay abreast of new de-

F I G U R E   5–4

Chally on Developing Technical Competencies

Willingness to Develop Technical Competencies	High Scores	Low Scores
• Driven to become expert on product applications and the key competencies required to function in the position. • Works to understand fully the principal technologies, processes, and methods of the business. • Maintains awareness of new product developments in their field.	• Wants to understand the most modern, state-of-the-art research and technology. • Continually asks questions to learn how things work, and to understand the underlying principles. • Routinely collects and reviews key data and information to track progress on all important functions. • Keeps up-to-date on technical or process knowledge.	• Tends to rely on others' expertise in areas in which he/she doesn't understand the technology or basic principles. • Can procrastinate and spend insufficient time tracking all key business information sources.

velopments in one's core competencies and to learn enough about related fields to apply knowledge effectively in the business (Figure 5–5).

George Bernard Shaw once said, "Those who cannot do, teach." It is more likely, however, that doers have a strong contribution to make—if they have the patience to show others how to do, thereby expanding their overall potential by working through others. Account managers who demonstrate a willingness to train and coach others understand the need for continued reinforcement of existing issues as well as presenting new concepts and ideas. They are comfortable taking responsibility for the group's continued learning and their motivation for the process. This skill is usually focused on formal sessions to provide information to a group to help them do their job more effectively.

FIGURE 5–5

Chally on Training Others

Training Others	High Scores	Low Scores
• Keeps the focus of training or education on improving others' effectiveness in meeting business goals and objectives. • Emphasizes those things that are the most useful to know and are going to make a difference to the individual being coached or educated.	• Committed to having an impact on others. • More concerned about results produced or change accomplished than with how attractive or entertaining the training can be. • Emphasizes activities that will help improve skills, focusing on efficiency of effort and eliminating irrelevant "fluff." • Concentrates on the three or four key issues that will make a difference in training people.	• Too concerned about detail, correctness, or other content issues. • May focus on making the training entertaining at the expense of making it informative. • May spend too much time in noncoaching activities developing elaborate training methods that do not provide added value.

Chally also came up with some working principles that correlate high-performing SAMs. Chally found they tend to believe the following points are critical:

- Learn how to meet and interact with your customers' top decision makers.

- Never take your competitors for granted; they'll usually surprise you.

- Set realistic goals, and be prepared for the stress of last-minute problems or changes that will come with no warning.

- Get to work before everybody else does.

- Know your customers' needs and concerns intimately.
- Help customers even in areas unrelated to your product or service.
- Only bend the rules when it's necessary to service the customer.
- Remember that competitors may sometimes offer better service.
- Make sure your customers know when a problem has been solved and that they know you know.

The "mind set" of less effective SAMs:

- The best thing about this job is the freedom it offers.
- I get so much information it's hard to keep up with it all.
- We could do better if we had better marketing materials.
- Marketing will keep us apprised of what the competition is doing.

Chally's competency model is one among many and we would strongly suggest researching which models might best apply to the expectations of your strategic accounts. The authors, with the help of a world-class practitioner panel, also developed a SAM competency model that provides another way of looking at the SAM's key competency categories.

THE S4 CONSULTING STRATEGIC ACCOUNT MANAGER COMPETENCY MODEL[4] CATEGORIES

We present these categories in descending order of importance, although all of them fit within six-tenths of a point on a five-point scale:

---

[4] © S4 Consulting, Inc.

- Show understanding of customer processes and industry.
- Develop and manage relationships.
- Show leadership.
- Use the consultative approach.
- Demonstrate entrepreneurial/intrepreneurial behavior.
- Show creative problem solving.
- Demonstrate ability to develop personal excellence.
- Demonstrate organizational skills.
- Think and act strategically.
- Execute the account management process.
- Demonstrate knowledge of supplier's processes and industry.

To determine whether a strategic account manager prospect has the competencies in these two models, more and more companies start with such a model and then develop and use creative behavioral interviewing in the selection process. Behavioral questions can allow you to gain real insights not only about what a candidate knows, but what a candidate can do. Consider the following behavioral questions for interviewing potential SAMs:

- Tell us about a time when you had to sell up an organizational hierarchy.
- Tell us about a time when you pulled together a cross-functional or multilevel team to accomplish a task successfully.
- Tell us about a time when you successfully sold an idea internally.
- Tell us about a time when your knowledge of the customer's needs saved the day.

These sorts of questions are very powerful and can generate responses that significantly reduce hiring errors in such a critical position.

HOW DO WE DEVELOP STRATEGIC ACCOUNT MANAGERS?

Once you have carefully selected a strategic account manager, how can you continue to develop that person's skills? How does someone learn to be a better SAM? As we saw above, some firms believe that little if any training is required if the person has sales skills. At the other extreme, though, are some firms with an unshakable belief that training alone will produce an account manager. This is the "training-as-silver-bullet" approach to developing account managers. But to assume that a few training programs alone (no matter how skillfully taught) will transform salespeople into account managers can be a very wasteful approach—especially if the firm is not making other investments in human-resource support.

Professional development is critical to creating skills and developing a strategic account manager's competencies. But in our experience, the most effective way to create and develop SAMs is for a firm to use high-performance selection criteria that mesh with the needs of the critical accounts. Some of the best of those suppliers actually have the customers interview the final two or three potential candidates to manage the customers' relationships. After the company hires account managers, they combine training, account assignment, compensation, and other human-resource support to drive behaviors that align with what the supplier needs and the accounts expect. Below is an example of a world-class organization wrestling with how to transition field salespeople into SAMs—a particularly thorny issue.

STRATEGIC ACCOUNT MANAGER TRAINING: THE MOTOROLA LMPS STORY

The story of Motorola Land Mobile Products Sector (LMPS), which successfully transitioned some sales representatives into SAMs, says a great deal about strategic account manager professional development and what else needs to occur if such training is going to be effective.

Motorola LMPS sells radios, mobile phones, and other communications devices to huge numbers of customers. In 1993, LMPS had 2,000+ sales reps serving 200,000 accounts. It was not uncommon for one sales rep to serve 250 accounts.

Problems started to develop with LMPS' market approach. Because they were spread so thin, reps were driven by their more needy customers to do service work. And the more service work they did, the fewer products they sold. LMPS found itself suffering from low sales productivity, high customer dissatisfaction, and increasing costs of sales. The situation became even more pressing when LMPS, through market research, validated what it had long suspected—roughly 20 percent of its customers were providing nearly 80 percent of its revenue.

LMPS began redesigning the way it approached its market. It first set up a dealer organization to serve the 80 percent of the customer base that generated 20 percent of its revenues. Then it reassigned most of the field salespeople. LMPS then identified its largest accounts (which it called "focused accounts") and assigned more than half its remaining salesforce to account teams dedicated to serving these accounts. The goal was that each representative/account manager would serve no more than six customers. These salespeople, who on average had been in their positions 10 years, almost overnight went from having hundreds of customers to just six. And here the challenges began to arise.

Before its restructuring, LMPS had defined sales rep productivity by each rep's total quarter-to-quarter sales activity. LMPS tracked rep performance by counting the number of appointments they set, the calls they made, the radios they sold, etc. Not surprisingly, reps thought their security depended on serving high numbers of customers. Given its strategic marketing shift, though, LMPS quickly changed all of its productivity measures. LMPS first changed its rep performance measures to the salesperson's knowledge of each customer and results per customer.

This shift and the new performance measures put the reps in totally unfamiliar positions. They knew how to get sales from a large number of customers by fulfilling short-term needs. They had never, however, been asked to design and implement a plan to penetrate a strategic account. LMPS corporate knew this. It also knew that if the sales reps were going to succeed, LMPS would have to help change the salespeople's old business model.

In a corporation famous for its commitment to learning, LMPS designed a training program that, among other things, taught reps how to conduct a situation appraisal, including how to: (1) conduct industry analyses, (2) do account analyses, and (3) write account plans. LMPS then told the salespeople to research their customers and their customers' industries. The problem was that many of the LMPS sales reps were not getting it. They didn't understand why they should spend two days in the library doing research and analysis. And their phones weren't ringing, which was the largest and most unsettling change of all.

LMPS had to show the representatives the possibilities of working intensely on just a few customers. As part of the initial account management training, LMPS distinguished between the old tactical and new strategic selling styles. For example, instead of selling 50 replacement radios at the request of a large customer's radio buyer, LMPS urged the rep to analyze the customer's entire communications plan. In many cases this was not easy because radio buyers didn't care about their firm's communications plan. They were simply following someone's orders to buy 50 new radios.

New account managers quickly realized that they would have to move the sale up in the customer organization to accomplish their goals. They simultaneously realized that they knew little about how to market to vice presidents. The account managers read books and studied strategic account management models, but it was hard for them to apply those models. As the reps continued to struggle, Motorola decided to approach the salespeople's transition more systematically.

First, LMPS created a business team to help transition the reps from hundreds of customers to only six accounts. After learning how IBM and Hewlett Packard had converted their salesforces, the team interviewed successful account managers from both IBM and HP. The team finally selected as LMPS' model for strategic account management the one that the Hewlett Packard rep had used to penetrate Motorola. The team found it very powerful that Motorola was one of HP's strategic accounts because LMPS people could see HP's presence at Motorola and could talk to the Motorola buyers about how HP was serving them.

The LMPS team also concluded that it would be necessary to create some experiential/simulation training to help the reps really understand strategic account management. This training focused on showing the reps their own future and what they could accomplish if they redefined their jobs. To build the simulation cases, LMPS interviewed a few LMPS reps that were very good at strategic account management. Five simulated accounts were developed based on five actual Motorola customers. The Motorola training design intended to simulate instances where the reps had to make choices that could either net them short-term gains or long-term opportunities.

The Motorola training design simulated instances where the reps had to make choices that could either net them short-term gains or long-term opportunities.

The training started with a three-day workshop in which each day—or "round"—stood for a year in the customer relationship. Trainees received presales and sales indicators to help them better understand their assigned relationship. Trainees did all the activities they would really do to manage the accounts, such as phone calls, negotiations, resource allocation, etc. Account teams underwent this training together so that the program could also act as a team builder. In each round, different but appropriate things happened in the customer relationships. At the end of each round, trainers provided feedback on how trainees' prior decision making had impacted the upcoming year with these customers.

The LMPS sales reps came in cocky the first day. They thought they could beat the simulations using their existing sales skills. In the first round, they sold all the radios they could. They usually achieved good revenue figures and mediocre profitability. In the second round, they lost their shirts because their short-term decisions in year one had eliminated most opportunities for year two. By lunchtime in round two, many reps were angry at the entire idea of the simulation. For some LMPS representatives, though, the simulations and focus on the customers' long-term needs provided a kind of conversion experience. They began to understand both the need for strategic account management and how they could use the approach to prosper. Not everyone, however, could redefine his job; some reps didn't make it.

After the workshop, the reps who graduated to becoming SAMs were given planning tools to use on the job. They used the repeatable sales process: (1) conducting a situation appraisal, (2) developing an account strategy, (3) implementing the action plan around that strategy, and (4) looking ahead to develop other strategies for growing the business. Each quarter they returned to account-review workshops in which they did account planning and reviewed their top three focused accounts before their peers. LMPS also conducted quarterly war-gaming workshops, in which account managers compared their account plans against those of the competition. One year after the first account managers completed the first three-day workshop, they returned for a follow-up simulation, during which account managers used actual customer evaluations as input for the fourth-year simulation.

The example we gave earlier about the Motorola LMPS rep who could have sold 50 replacement radios or conduct an analysis of the customer's whole communications plan (in search of larger opportunities) was real. After the account manager went through the training and returned to analyze that account's communications plan, she and two team members held a meeting with three VP-level customer contacts and the plant general manager to report their findings. When she was done, the most senior customer VP said, "There are four people in this room who really know our business and three of them are from Motorola." The meeting resulted in a $500,000 order. The customer has since installed Motorola systems in seven additional plants.

Before it finally succeeded, LMPS systematically grappled with a number of variables: performance measurements, team building, compensation, the need to demonstrate new business models and approaches to very experienced salespeople, and sales manager coaching after the program.

These results were not atypical. Since the LMPS simulation training was introduced, the productivity of LMPS representatives has tripled, and both customer and employee satisfaction ratings have shown exceptional improvement.

The point here is not simply to present a creative way to turn sales representatives into SAMs. Instead, Motorola LMPS, having started the transition, quickly realized that training the reps was only one part of the puzzle. Before it finally succeeded, LMPS systematically grappled with a number of variables: performance measurements, team building, compensation, the need to demonstrate new business models and approaches to very experienced salespeople, and sales manager coaching after the program.

LMPS quickly learned training alone wouldn't allow the reps to succeed. Motorola LMPS carefully addressed the human-resource support that needed to be changed if their account managers were going to succeed. And succeed they did.

HOW DO WE ASSIGN STRATEGIC ACCOUNT MANAGERS?

Some firms simply do not understand—as Motorola did—the need to concentrate strategic account management on a small number of accounts. We became aware of the problem in the early nineties, when we created a 36-member world-class strategic account manager panel. We periodically submitted research questions to this panel. In 1995, one of our consultants asked several panel members how many customers a strategic account manager could effectively manage. The panel members responded by telling the consultant he was asking the wrong question—he should be asking how many individual relationships an account manager should manage. The consultant then asked that question to our entire panel.

It seemed to us that, with the answer to this and other questions, we could construct an account-manager staffing analog, a tool we had not seen before. Among other questions, our consultant asked the panel how much time each month a relationship required to prevent "drift," where the customer, not feeling enough attention from the supplier, simply drifts toward another supplier relationship. He also asked strategic accounts how often they needed to see an account manager. To our surprise, given the many industries and account managers replying, accounts and panel members agreed that individual relationship management took an average time of somewhere between two and eight hours a month. The two to eight hours is not necessarily face time. It could be phone time or email. It depends on the expectation of the strategic account contacts and the maturity of the relationship. New relationships tend to take more time; older relationships, once you establish reliability and trust, tend to take less time. This of course depends on any given account contact's relationship needs (Figure 5–6).

Starting with the 2 to 8 hours a month needed to prevent drift, we can begin to construct a strategic account management assignment model based not on sales models but on the expectations of account contacts. The model assumes that there are 20 workdays in a month, or 160 hours—although

F I G U R E   5–6

Things to Consider

1. Strategic accounts have multiperson relationships, and require that a minimum of 5 to 10 relationships be managed.
2. Effective account managers need to manage a number of internal relationships as well.

most account managers thought this assumption laughable. One said, "We're on flex time here . . . I can work any 90 hours a week I want to." If you accept those two assumptions, though, a strategic account manager really has time to manage between 20 and 80 individual relationships. Account managers consistently told us, however, that the ideal number of relationships to manage was somewhere between 40 and 60, although most did admit to being responsible for at least 60 to 80 relationships. So their responses were consistent with each other. When we asked some account managers on the panel how they were handling the last 20 individual relationships, most said they were concentrating on the higher-leverage account contacts. In other words, they were skimming some of the account contact relationships.

Companies tend to compensate employees based on the ease and efficiency of internal processing rather than on exceeding the expectations of strategic accounts.

This model also assumes that SAMs will have to manage a number of *internal* relationships if they are consistently going to exceed account expectations. This is especially critical at suppliers just starting strategic account programs, where alignment may not have occurred. But even if the strategic account management program is 10 years old, we have mentioned before how many suppliers' delivery systems, processes, and therefore employees are internally focused.

Companies tend to compensate employees based on the ease and efficiency of internal processing rather than on exceeding the expectations of strategic accounts.

In unaligned firms, SAMs sometimes spend the bulk of their time selling to and managing internal relationships. Such internal marketing is almost never a value-added activity for the strategic account manager.

So from the 20 to 80 individual relationships, subtract 10 to 20 from the number of external relationships, to make room for internal relationships—not a high number when considering the layers, levels, and internal orientation of most large suppliers. Now we are down to one account manager "owning" 10 to 60 individual external relationships, which is within the ideal number of 40 to 60 relationships our panel mentioned.

The model's final assumption is that key account relationships are "many-headed"—with a minimum of 5 or 10 contacts with which relationships need to be developed and managed—and this could be too low a number for some of your larger relationships. Let's look at our competed equation graphically (Figure 5–7).[5]

That translates the 10 to 60 relationships into 1 to 12 accounts. Keep in mind that 1 to 12 accounts tends to be low for

F I G U R E   5–7

Potential # of Manageable Relationships (20–80)
MINUS (–)
Potential # of Internal Relationships (10–20)
EQUALS (=)
Potential # of External Relationships (10–60)
DIVIDED BY (÷)
Potential # of Relationships per Account (5–10)
EQUALS (=)
Potential # of Accounts Assigned to One Account Manager (1–12)

[5] ©S4 Consulting, Inc.

most people called strategic account managers. We recommend that you adjust this model for your own program (many strategic account relationships, for example, require that substantially more than 5 to 10 relationships be managed). Many firms—as we did at first—are asking the wrong questions in assigning SAMs.

Overassigning accounts is one of the fastest ways to nullify the effectiveness of an excellent account manager.

A number of factors can impact the final number—that a strategic account manager should be managing 1 to 12 accounts (Figure 5–8).

Again and again, lost-account interviews reveal that the ex-supplier had badly underestimated the time relationship management required. Overassigning accounts—unfortunately commonplace in account manage-

---

F I G U R E   5 – 8

Factors Impacting Strategic Account Assignment

1. How much opportunity does a given customer offer?

2. How experienced is the account manager?

3. Is the customer geographically dispersed?

4. Is decision making decentralized?

5. How many individual relationships need to be managed at the strategic accounts?

6. How well aligned is the supplier?

7. Has a huge new opportunity suddenly appeared that requires a seasoned strategic account manager?

8. How many supplier employees and executives are willing and able to support these relationship-management activities?

9. Will employees outside sales take responsibility for tasks assigned them by the strategic account manager?

10. Are there sufficient support people so that the large account managers can concentrate on value creation and relationship management rather than purely sales or administrative duties?

ment—is one of the fastest ways to nullify the effectiveness of an excellent account manager.

There are holes in this model. It allows no time for at least four major account management activities: (1) account planning (which our panel stated was one of the three most time-consuming tasks performed by excellent SAMs), (2) administrative activity (reporting and control), (3) travel time, and (4) vacation/personal time. We readily admit that these holes lower still further the number of customer relationships an account manager can manage.

We would argue, however, that this staffing analog, even with its holes, is far closer to account-defined reality than any headcount projection or sales-staffing model.

It continues to surprise us how many suppliers make critical staffing decisions not on what their strategic accounts expect or merit but on staffing analogs whose relation to reality is statistical at best. The point of this exercise is not exactitude as much as it is to achieve account focus: to start seeing strategic account management from the customers' point of view.

We've spoken about the challenges of SAM selection, development, and assignment. Let's now turn our attention to the challenge of account manager compensation.

HOW DO WE PAY STRATEGIC ACCOUNT MANAGERS?

There are many potential pitfalls with strategic account manager compensation. The two that we believe have the most power to kill the program are (1) how the account manager compensation is balanced between salary and any short-term incentives and (2) whether the strategic account manager is compensated in such a way that field salespeople and internal employees will find it worthwhile to help the manager, the customer, and the program.

First, when SAM compensation is heavily weighted toward short-term incentives, account managers tend to ignore all things strategic or long-term and focus on generating new business. And who could blame them? That is where their payoff lies. Compensation drives behavior; short-term compensation drives short-term transactional thinking and selling—not strategic account management.

Strategic account manager compensation is most often balanced 75 to 85 percent salary and 15 to 25 percent incentive bonus.

Our experience, echoed by the annual SAM compensation study conducted by the Strategic Account Management Association, has been that strategic account manager compensation is most often balanced 75 to 85 percent salary and 15 to 25 percent incentive bonus.

The salary usually includes explicit revenue-growth goals that strategic account planners develop. Incentives might include hitting certain account share or profitability targets, or creating longer-term strategic initiatives. This compensation allows the account manager to concentrate on longer-term strategic solutions, which also tend to be larger and more profitable.

The other potential compensation pitfall is how the strategic account manager's compensation impacts that of the field salespeople and operations folks, an area account management programs designers too seldom consider. One firm serving a multilocation strategic account hired an account manager from outside the firm and paid her 50 percent salary and 50 percent commission. She assumed responsibility for eight large strategic relationships. As is typical, though, she depended on the field salespeople to manage and service the strategic accounts' local relationships. Everyone agreed this made sense. The supplier, however, did not want to descend into the briar patch that is sales compensation and decided that the account manager and the field salesperson should split the commission on any incremental sales. As is the case with most pitfalls, this made sense only in theory.

Three basic field responses to the compensation change emerged, only one of which was positive. In the first field response, salespeople started spending less time at the strategic account because they could earn full commissions by serving nonstrategic accounts. This meant certain field salespeople devoted less attention to strategic account locations than they had before the program existed.

In the second scenario, the field salespeople sold to the strategic account and then went after their full commission by arguing their case to their regional vice president. In several cases, the highly autonomous regional vice presidents had initiated the strategic relationship and didn't like to see their power taken over by the strategic account program, particularly by an "outsider." They therefore let their salespeople earn their full commission, dealing the account manager and the program serious blows. And because of the time this arguing and refereeing required, certain account locations received less attention.

The third scenario was rare but deserves mention. A few field salespeople (out of 100+) saw what was possible in a strategic account management program. They worked with the account manager to realize that potential. In several cases, these salespeople, some of whom were relatively low performers in field selling, later became effective strategic account managers.

Now let's examine a particularly thorny case from IBM Global, which faced the account manager-field compensation problem in its global account management program and came up with an ingenious interim solution.

THE IBM GLOBAL STORY

IBM's global account manager compensation story starts with IBM's largest customers, who began requiring more consistent global sourcing from its suppliers. In the early 1990s, this was particularly difficult for IBM because of its geographical organization. At that time, if the account was located in your area, it was your responsibility and you got paid for it. For example, Ford Motor Company was very well supported in Dearborn, Michigan, but people in other territories had no incentive to contribute to Ford—either in Dearborn or in Europe. A large number of IBM executives realized that this geographic structure was not really helping the strategic account, which didn't really care how IBM was organized. One executive said, "Customers don't care how IBM does it. They cut a check and they tell IBM to go forth and conquer. It shouldn't matter how it's done, just that *it is done*."

Lou Gerstner, IBM's president, heard the customers' clamoring and realized IBM was going to have to provide a more coordinated global response to their needs. In May 1994, Gerstner reorganized IBM into 13 industry groups. For example, a manufacturing group serving Ford is independent of any geographic boundaries. IBM also changed the way it managed global accounts, naming employees in direct customer contact positions "worldwide client executives (WCE's)" and assigning them dedicated support staff. For example, IBM's Ford WCE has salespeople, project managers, and technical people who work directly for him on the Ford account. He also has responsibility for others who are matrixed onto the Ford team. These people have someone else as their official boss, but they work on Ford 100 percent of the time.

Soon after the reorganization, though, problems arose when the WCE's would request assistance for their customer from remote IBM locations. Because there was little consistency in how the country managers handled their compensation programs, there was usually little incentive for either the country managers or the remote IBM employees to assist the global account manager—even if the account were huge. This inconsistency created a disconnect between the WCEs' goals and those of the remote field people, leaving customers trapped among warring compensation systems. Gerstner and IBM realized that they would need to change the IBM global compensation structure so everyone would be headed in roughly the same direction.

IBM and consultants started working with a select group of IBM employees to consider possible compensation plans to rectify this problem. IBM's Ford WCE and several of his Ford team members participated in the compensation redesign sessions. At first, the North American and European teams went through simulations on paper. This provided an opportunity to work out the problems before IBM rolled out the new compensation plan.

IBM's new compensation plan recognized that people on teams such as those serving Ford have some incentive compensation tied to team goals. IBM therefore gave the WCE partial control over team members' variable compensation incentives. They could, for example, set up specific incentives for services teams or product specialists that contribute to the strategic account relationship. Client executives can specify the measures and the dollar amount of the incentive. For example, a product specialist who was previously paid to push IBM technology was then rewarded for encouraging the best solution for the customer, regardless of whose technology the solution requires. Any product specialist who doesn't sell the best solution doesn't maximize her personal earnings. They left money on the table if they were not working with the whole team. It was a subjective measure, but it worked.

That was creative but the truly innovative component of IBM's global compensation plan was the personal business contribution (PBC) bonuses. The worldwide client executive could offer a bonus to any IBM employee in the world who contributed to developing the worldwide client relationship. For example, IBM's Ford WCE can ask German employees to do something for Ford and can offer those employees 500 Euros for their contributions. He can create discrete activities and support them with direct pay. On top of this, remote IBM executives received

variable pay based on the corporate and geographic performance of the company. This compensation provided incentives
for the remote executives and employees to work for relationships on whose financial future IBM depended.

IBM's global compensation system moved from a regional
to a customer focus, regardless of that customer's location. The
sales compensation plans for IBM's large accounts are now consistent across the world, with only slight variations based on regional legalities. IBM executives described the compensation
system as a form of "global plumbing that ties us all together to
get work done for our customers."

IBM's global compensation program allows IBM to service its strategic accounts from a truly global perspective. This
benefit, in turn, has contributed to increased business for IBM.

The European Ford team's pay depends on global revenue
created from Ford. An English IBM employee will now choose
to come on board to help with some local Ford issue because
they easily understand their incentive to do so. IBM's Ford account posted its best year ever in 1995. This was attributed, in
large part, to the new compensation program. IBM had $30 mil-
lion to $40 million in additional business from Ford alone dur-
ing 1995. Ford was so impressed with IBM's service quality that
it asked IBM to treat Mazda as a Ford entity.

IBM believed strongly that the underlying structure of its
new compensation program was very sound, and it wanted to
keep the program as simple as possible. Consequently, IBM did
not impose many changes on the program in the late 1990s. IBM
then worked out a way to let the various organizations within
IBM know how it pays people throughout the whole company.
It built templates that illustrate how it rewards particular positions. By January 1, 1997, the compensation plan, including
these templates, was on IBM's intranet for everyone at IBM
across the globe to examine. And in 1996 IBM paid out $1 billion
to employees in variable pay.

Team-based compensation is one of the most problemati-
cal areas in strategic account management, worthy of several
books. For team-based compensation to work, you need very
specific individual objectives that, together, add up to total ac-

count success. The variables in this scenario are geometric. Firms can fail if the individual goals are hazy or if the individual objectives are not based on performance. You need to think through any team-based compensation very carefully because it can potentially increase your cost of sales without driving additional revenues and profits.

IBM's revolutionary program recognized the importance of a boundary-less organization for its global accounts and was willing to pay for it with cash and political capital. IBM moved toward a model in which the worldwide client executive is basically the CEO of a strategic account business unit who can pay employees for their efforts on a given account.

IBM's story makes a strong case for creating a compensation program that drives strategic account managers to treat their assigned relationships as their own strategic business units.

IBM's story makes a strong case for creating a compensation program that drives strategic account managers to treat their assigned relationships as their own strategic business units.

The SAM thus becomes a general manager of her assigned customers, accountable for balancing the relationships' short-term cash flow with their long-term profitability (as was the case with Honeywell Industrial Automation and Control Solutions).

CREATE HUMAN RESOURCES SUPPORT FOR STRATEGIC ACCOUNT MANAGERS

How can you ensure that your firm has created human-resources support for strategic account managers?

1. Select and develop strategic account managers based on a validated set of account manager competencies.

2. Assign strategic account managers based on the number of account relationships to be managed rather than on the number of accounts.

3. Develop a repeatable yet flexible sales process for your strategic account managers.

4. Create account manager compensation programs that drive long-term strategic relationship building by striking a balance between salary (75 to 85 percent) and incentive-bonus plans (15 to 25 percent) that reward the account manager for achieving strategic, relationship, and revenue goals.

CHAPTER 6

Key 5: Create Firmwide Relationships at Multiple Levels of Relationships between the Firm and Its Most Critical Accounts

In this chapter we focus on creating and managing interfirm relationships with strategic accounts. We will be discussing:

1. Mapping strategic account relationships.
2. The strategic account loss cycle.
3. Preventing the strategic account loss cycle.

Often sellers focus on developing and maintaining strong relationships with tactical customer employees, such as purchasing people and technicians. While it is important to develop such relationships, the strategic account manager (SAM) should develop firmwide relationships—ongoing parallel linkages between functional areas of the supplier and account. We like to call it "covering the bases." Unless the relationship is firmwide, with the account manager acting as a liaison between customer needs and supplier resources, savvy competitors will have a great opportunity to woo away critical decision makers.

For example, a key account salesperson was promoted to strategic account manager because he had successfully worked with the customer for seven years and had an excellent relationship with the purchasing manager. They had golfed and hunted together. But on a quarterly call, the new SAM arrived to find a very unhappy friend. The purchasing manager told him that a competitor had been in, had scheduled, and had made several presentations to three executives. The executives found the competitor's overall value compelling and had simply told the purchasing person to start buying from the new supplier. The account manager, who had seen little reason to speak with these executives, was stunned—as were the executives to whom he reported.

Unless the relationship is firmwide, with the account manager acting as a liaison between customer needs and supplier resources, savvy competitors will have a great opportunity to woo away critical decision makers.

The account manager's hard-won lesson was that he needed to create and manage multiple and multilevel relationships in each strategic account. If your strategic account management efforts do not include identifying and managing influencers in the buying group, you may be playing customer roulette.

Basic selling know-how is the key to initiating a firmwide relationship. Covering the bases, understanding the buying process and decision makers (or as we like to call them, "buying influences") requires: (1) identifying all of the influences for a given opportunity, (2) understanding each influence's role, and (3) pinpointing his or her degree of influence over the decision.

At a high level, these are the sorts of roles you are looking for:

Economic Buyers can give final approval to buy. They can say "yes" when everyone else has said "no," as well as veto a deal that everyone else has approved.

User Buyers use or supervise the use of your product or service. Their personal success typically is tied to the success of your solution.

Technical Buyers judge the measurable, quantifiable aspects of your proposal. They may act as gatekeepers and can say "no" to a proposal based on specs or technical issues.

Coaches want your solution for a particular opportunity and act as a guide by providing information you need to position yourself effectively with each buying influence, and ultimately close business. Coaches must be proactively identified and developed.[1]

Figure 6–1 shows a model of a buying influence group map, superimposed over an organizational chart

Understanding and mapping the buying influences may at first seem fairly simple, but that may be misleading if the account manager has missed or misinterpreted a role. We recall a gifted national account manager for a truck-component manufacturer who was selling to a large fleet for more than seven months. His experience told him the economic buyer had to be the fleet's VP of sales or VP of marketing. One day the VP of sales asked him why he was pushing the benefits to him when the VP of purchasing was the decision maker. This was news to him. Had he known the VP of purchasing's role earlier, he could have more effectively leveraged his selling time. After he verified the group's roles, he was able to complete a huge sale in several months. But he had never seen a VP of purchasing who acted as an economic decision maker.

Optimized time, though, is only one of the benefits of a buying-influence group map. The map is also a communication tool—a roadmap to the relationship structure that enables even a new account manager to figure out where to start. In our experience, too many strategic account managers either don't have a handle on the customer's buying influences or they do not share that account knowledge (a huge asset) with others. Such unshared information almost always negatively impacts the customer relationship.

---

[1] ©Miller Heiman, Inc.

FIGURE 6-1

Buying Influence Group (BIG) Map

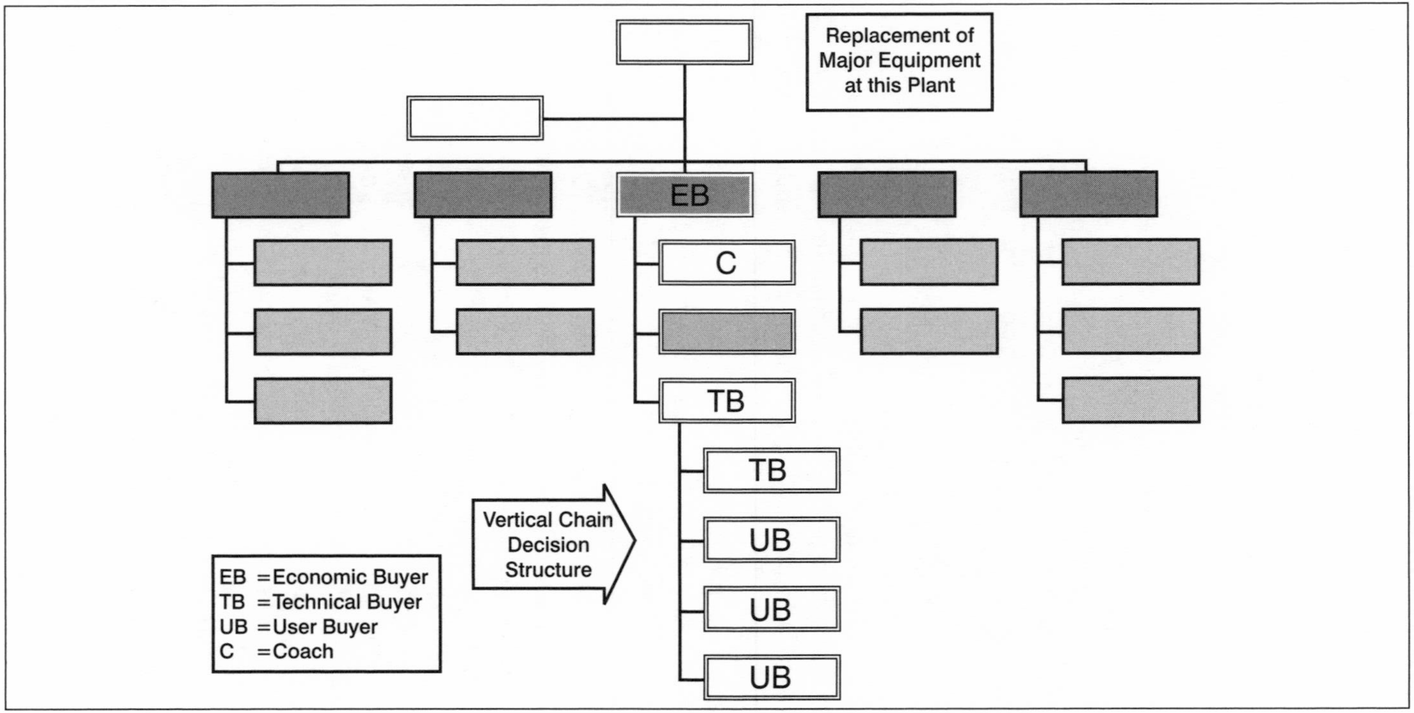

Replacement of
Major Equipment
at this Plant

EB

C

TB

TB

UB

UB

UB

Vertical Chain
Decision
Structure

EB = Economic Buyer
TB = Technical Buyer
UB = User Buyer
C = Coach

Another key point here. We are not saying that the account manager will herself manage all these relationships, which in some cases can number several dozen. A good strategic account manager may initiate these relationships, but managing them day-to-day may be a task for appropriate supplier executives/managers—one of the parallel linkages mentioned earlier. These executives/managers need to know the customers' respective account plans cold and must develop personal objectives based on the supplier's goals for the accounts. The SAM can step in as a resource when needed but the executives/managers will ideally manage that personal relationship. To manage this many relationships, the firm will ideally create an easily accessible repository of ongoing contact information from previous customer communication. This repository might even include an executive's parenthetical comments about the call, which can signal a huge opportunity to another member of the supplier account team. The wider and deeper the chain of effectively managed relationships, the higher the account's emotional costs of switching to another supplier.

The wider and deeper the chain of effectively managed relationships, the higher the account's emotional costs of switching to another supplier.

So, after mapping the buying influences, we suggest that account managers validate their information. On the next two pages we present tools for SAMs to think more deeply about customers they have identified in the buying influence group.

RELATIONSHIP MAP CHECKLIST[2]

In Figure 6–2 is a checklist to validate the buying influence group map. These questions should lead SAMs to take a hard look at their relationships within accounts.

---

[2]   ©S4 Consulting, Inc.

Relationship Map Checklist

Customer Manager	Customer					
Name						
Title						
Role in decision group: • Economic Buyer • User Buyer • Technical Buyer • Coach						
How do you know their role?						
What motivates this individual? To what need should I sell?						
Their top three needs?						
How do you know?						
Their preferred means of communication . . . • Face-to-face • Phone • Email • Other?						
Their desired frequency of contact?						
How do you know?						
Their primary contact						
How could I—or someone else—deepen this relationship?						

A very creative director of strategic accounts used this Buying Influence Map Checklist at a national sales meeting. He first asked that his account managers fill out the sheet for one of their most critical customers. He then had each manager present how his customer "worked" to two other people in the group. The real things you need to learn from your people—and this tool can help greatly—are:

1. Which part of the worksheet, if any, did you have the most difficulty completing? Why?

2. Was there anything you thought you knew and now wonder if you do?

3. What insights emerged as you went through this exercise?

4. What additional information about your customer, if any, do you believe it now would be helpful to have?

A caution about the worksheet: strategic account managers may be tempted to fly through the "How do you know?" questions. These are harder than they may initially seem. Just as the SAM earlier "knew" the VP of purchasing couldn't be the economic decision maker, so many strategic account managers take their gut feel as gospel. This question allows them to examine their assumptions (a manager's coaching can be very helpful here). After completing this exercise, many SAMs realize they do not know their account's buying influences as well as they thought they did.

THE STRATEGIC ACCOUNT LOSS CYCLE

During the last 16 years, we have interviewed thousands of decision makers, including a large number at lost strategic accounts. As we conducted those interviews, certain patterns began to emerge in how customer relationships end. We were able to identify some root causes for those relationships dying. The graph in Figure 6–3 illustrates our conclusions.

F I G U R E   6–3

Strategic Account Loss Cycle

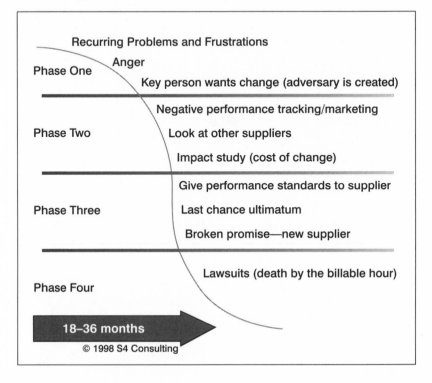

Phase One   Recurring Problems and Frustrations
             Anger
             Key person wants change (adversary is created)

Phase Two   Negative performance tracking/marketing
             Look at other suppliers
             Impact study (cost of change)

Phase Three Give performance standards to supplier
             Last chance ultimatum
             Broken promise—new supplier

Phase Four   Lawsuits (death by the billable hour)

18–36 months

© 1998 S4 Consulting

Phase One: Not surprisingly, the strategic account loss cycle starts with recurring problems and customer frustration. In many cases, phase one can result from not covering your bases, not following up, not truly understanding an account's needs, or not seeing that recurring account complaints shield a more serious issue. These issues tend to lead to not once-in-a-while problems (that can appear almost any time in a relationship), but problems that occur increasingly often and can negatively impact some critical account contact's performance measurement. Supplier shipments might be delivered late, leading to line slowdowns or even stoppages. There may be a recurring product-quality problem. Whatever the recurring problem, when an account employee gets docked for the supplier's poor performance, he starts to complain to the supplier, and when that poor performance continues, he (or she) gets angry and very focused, and becomes an adversary. This is a solid reason for setting up supplier performance-measurement systems at the account.

A company we know wanted to assess relationships with critical customers. These assessments included a customer win/loss analysis. We asked this company whether it had lost a major customer in the last five years. After some very loud silence, a supplier executive nodded and said, "But she won't talk to you." It turned out the firm had lost a top-three customer three years before—primarily through the internal efforts of a customer production supervisor, an overlooked user buyer. The supervisor had lost her bonus because the supplier's poor shipping performance caused major blips in line utilization.

We then called the supervisor and asked if she would be willing to answer some questions about the supplier. After a very long pause, she asked one question, "Are they paying you by the hour?" When she was told "yes," she invited us to her office and spoke for six hours. Those six hours were among the study's most valuable to the supplier because she gave detailed information regarding the firm's poor performance, failed processes, and failed systems. The incident was painful for the supplier to relive but it pointed out processes that remained ineffective and that other accounts had been complaining about.

Phase Two: Once negative supplier performance has burned a customer, adversaries feel a personal mission—a calling—to rid themselves and their company of the offending supplier. Thus begins phase two, in which the adversary starts tracking negative performance to condemn the supplier. One critical lesson: if a strategic supplier does not quickly develop systems to measure critical performance indicators at an account, the adversary will set up systems that track the supplier's lack of performance.

Armed with lack-of-performance metrics, the customer adversary then becomes a VP of negative internal marketing for the supplier, giving regular short marketing presentations as to why the supplier should no longer serve his firm. We once spoke to an executive customer contact who was very unhappy with a supplier. He reached over to his bookcase and pulled down a six-slide, multicolored, graph-filled presentation about the supplier's shortcomings. He gave the 10-minute presentation so professionally that it was clear he had had a great deal of practice. You do not have to be a marketing professional to see this as a very bad sign for the supplier.

Armed with lack-of-performance metrics, the customer adversary then becomes a VP of negative internal marketing for the supplier . . .

Over time the adversary, at whatever management level, starts to develop a group that supports his position and is willing to look at other suppliers. If the supplier is a service organization and switchover costs are minimal, the customer might switch suppliers now, during phase two. If supplier switchover requires major changes, such as retooling a manufacturing line, the adversary usually will aim to fund an impact study to compare the cost of change to the cost of continuing to do business with the supplier.

Phase Three: The sorts of momentum an existing supplier relationship can have intrigue us. In most cases, after the adversary completes the impact study, an executive at the customer will turn to her counterpart at the supplier and provide baseline performance standards and demand that the supplier meet them. Usually the poor-performance report shocks the supplier's executives, because internal account managers may have carefully insulated the executives from the firm's poor performance.

In these cases, supplier executives tend to act in depressingly similar fashions. They go to the areas that are underperforming—shipping, say—and demand that they improve performance if they want to keep their jobs. Performance will minimally improve, but if the problem has been recurring, there is almost always some process or system out of alignment with the customer's expectations. Saber rattling does not redesign systems or processes, so the problem persists. This usually leads to the customer flinging an ultimatum at the supplier, which leads to another flare-up of executive rhetoric, and then to a broken promise and new supplier.

Phase Four: Although this phase on the graph seems to be part of a linear progression, phase four of the loss cycle only happens in about 1 out of every 30 customer losses. In those cases liability issues are involved and the customer hurls not just demands but lawsuits. In most cases the supplier hurls back countersuits and there can be a lengthy legal battle, in which the winners are sometimes only the lawyers. Such a suit can potentially kill the supplier. It is one thing to lose a large customer's revenue stream; it is quite another to lose that *and* a treble-damage liability suit and have your firm's margin wiped out for years.

PREVENTING THE STRATEGIC ACCOUNT LOSS CYCLE

The loss cycle highlights the need to capture an in-depth relationship map of the buyer-influence group, including the top three goals of each member. It also strengthens the case for creating parallel linkages between firms, linkages that can hold the overall relationship together even if one of them starts to weaken. In most cases, adversaries are born because the supplier is not carefully managing all critical relationships—not covering the bases. This can happen because the account manager is overassigned and has to "skim" some relationships. But it can also happen simply because the account manager did not learn the correct role or the critical goals and challenges of a buyer influence. In our experience firms rarely set up performance measurement systems based on the expectations of buyer influences. But those firms that do tend to have much longer and more successful relationships with strategic accounts. Below is the example of U.S. West's Vicki Towey, who determined her account's real needs and measured her performance by the hassles she was able to help her customer avoid.

THE U.S. WEST/DAYTON HUDSON STORY

In 1999 U.S. West (now a part of Qwest Communications), was an $11 billion telecommunications company that served more than 25 million customers in 14 states, including residential, small- and medium-sized businesses, federal, education, Internet service providers, and large customers. In 1999 U.S. West served 32 strategic accounts that generated $400 million, or 30 to 40 percent of U.S. West's revenue from large industrial and commercial businesses. Twelve senior account managers served the largest of these strategic accounts (Dayton Hudson Corporation, Wells-Fargo, Boeing, etc.). For four years Vicki Towey had been the SAM for Dayton Hudson, the retailing giant (Dayton's, Hudson's, Mervyn's, Target Stores) based in Minneapolis. It was a complex job at which she excelled.

In 1999 Towey estimated that she was maintaining or orchestrating more than 60 relationships at Dayton Hudson—at all levels of the organization. She spent a great deal of time working with Dayton Hudson's operations people, its planners, the firm's managers, and executives. Managing multiple relationships, she said, allowed her to determine what was keeping both middle and upper managers awake at night. It also allowed her to determine Dayton Hudson's strategic and day-to-day business needs—in many cases before Dayton Hudson fully realized those needs.

In the mid-to-late nineties, Dayton Hudson was undergoing the pain of consolidating three autonomous divisions' information systems & communications infrastructure. At the same time, Dayton Hudson was planning to build a 14-story office tower in downtown Minneapolis. Dayton Hudson employees at many levels confided in Towey that they were not looking forward to a similarly complex task of designing and managing the IT and communications infrastructure for the new building.

The task was complex because it required managing the multiple suppliers needed to establish the routes through which voice, video, and data flow in an organization. This communications infrastructure can involve hundreds of services, all of which need to smoothly work together and most of which need to be easily accessible from the employee's desktop. For Dayton Hudson's new building, the required services included E-commerce, fiber-optic cabling, voice, video, and data services, LAN switching services, WAN connectivity, disaster recovery services, and work-at-home portfolios—just to name a few. Each of these services was offered by multiple vendors, which meant that in a given project someone had to manage dozens of suppliers so everything came together on time and under budget.

But where Dayton Hudson saw a major hassle, Towey saw a major opportunity: to gain the majority of the communications-infrastructure design business by becoming accountable for those hassles. She would bundle all the necessary services by acting as a general contractor for the design and development of the Dayton Hudson building's communications infrastructure. When Dayton Hudson sent the RFP out, Towey believed she had a major opportunity to apply the knowledge and relationships she had developed over nine years to capture the lion's share of the business. She said she "wanted to own the desktops" at the new Dayton Hudson office tower. When Dayton Hudson sent the project out to bid, it narrowed the choices down to 20 suppliers, then 8 suppliers, and then 1 (U.S. West).

Dayton Hudson chose U.S. West because of the unique service bundle that Towey and her team had structured. Essentially, Towey had translated all the concerns voiced to her by Dayton Hudson middle and upper management into a customized bundled solution. U.S. West would act as the general manager for designing and developing the communications infrastructure (voice, video, data), assuming responsibility for project management and offering competitive flat labor rates for most of the required tasks. This meant that Dayton Hudson would not have to deal with multiple communications infrastructure vendors, only with U.S. West. With the resources allocated and ready, service-level agreements and technical specifications drawn up, U.S. West started delivering its Dayton Hudson "service delivery partnership solution."

The number of services bundled was so great that, in many cases, the products Dayton Hudson bought were not U.S. West's. For example, Dayton Hudson bought a switch from one of U.S. West's major competitors, but the competitor simply installed the switch and then U.S. West installed all peripheral equipment (sets) at the flat labor rates, saving Dayton Hudson significant costs in the process. Towey continued to manage internal relationships, introducing U.S. West and subcontractors to her Dayton Hudson contacts and making sure that the project went smoothly. She says that at this point she spent a great deal of time "keeping all the balls in the air." Towey's solution allowed Dayton Hudson to do what they did best—retailing—and allowed U.S. West to assume the total project management accountability for infrastructure design and development, and to reap the rewards for so doing. It was one of those times when supplier performance was easily judged and tracked: was Dayton Hudson having to assume any of the communications infrastructure hassles, and did that infrastructure allow the effective delivery of video, voice, and data?

Dayton Hudson estimated that U.S. West's "service-delivery partnership solution" saved it millions of dollars. And customer satisfaction was never higher. In 1998 Dayton Hudson's Executive Vice President and CIO Vivian Stephenson awarded U.S. West its DH CIS' Best Business Partner Award. As Stephenson said in her award letter, "These awards recognize vendors who have achieved excellence in service, leadership, and execution."

There are also major benefits for U.S. West. First, the contract generated $5 million in incremental business. Second, because U.S. West designed the building's technical specifications and installed the vast majority of hardware and software, U.S. West knows the building and its communications infrastructure better than anyone and will be providing technical assistance, including dedicated on-site technicians, for many years. Third, Dayton Hudson was about to begin an even bigger project, a new 32-story corporate headquarters building in Minneapolis. No firm was better positioned than U.S. West to develop that building's communications infrastructure—and

U.S. West again won the bid and its $10 to $15 million incremental revenue. Without the 60+ relationships and deep knowledge of Dayton Hudson challenges, Towey would not have been able to identify the opportunity. Without her project management abilities and her support folks, she would not have been able to take advantage of the opportunity. Towey's success positioned her and U.S. West for even more business from Dayton Hudson. Deep customer knowledge and firmwide relationships led to huge dollar paybacks for both supplier and customer.

Such in-depth relationships and account knowledge also led 3M in its success with IBM Storage, which we describe below.

THE 3M/IBM STORAGE STORY

IBM Storage makes giant magnetic resistive recording heads (GMR heads) for computer hard drives. Jan Hildebrandt, the 3M account manager for IBM Storage, first worked to gain an in-depth relationship with the firm so she could understand its business challenges. She established multiple relationships—from executive VP to procurement—at IBM Storage's design centers in San Jose, California and Fujisawa, Japan, and at IBM corporate, where she began to understand more clearly how IBM Storage fit into IBM's global marketing strategy.

By working closely with IBM's design and manufacturing teams in California and Japan, Hildebrandt identified one of IBM Storage's largest business problems: GMR heads are extremely sensitive to electrostatic discharge created during the manufacturing process, which can result in up to 25 to 30 percent product loss. Hildebrandt brought in 3M's Technology Group, which helped redesign the GMR head manufacturing process with less static-sensitive materials. Through those efforts, 3M reduced IBM Storage's GMR product-yield loss by 10 percent, which translates to several million dollars annually. Hildebrandt coordinated the various 3M resources required at the San Jose IBM design facility.

The GMR effort was so successful that IBM Storage came to consider Jan Hildebrandt and the 15 3M technology organizations she represented (electrostatic, filtration, adhesion, etc.) as critical resources and strategic partners, particularly when IBM encountered customized-production problems.

When IBM Storage identified such a problem, it came to Hildebrandt in the early stages to see if 3M resources could help. 3M found itself modifying some of its existing products or combining existing technologies to create new products to support IBM's needs.

3M sales to IBM Storage increased 300 percent in two years—or more than $10 million in incremental dollars. When the IBM executives with whom she had established relationships saw the results she had delivered, 3M was very well positioned for further partnering efforts. Sales increased more than 25 percent in 2001, partially through three new partnering opportunities that Hildebrandt helped identify.

She had developed executive relationships at corporate and at the various sites, she identified problems that her 3M technology partners could solve, and she coordinated those projects to ensure IBM received the value-added.

In both these cases, the SAM started by developing multiple relationships with her customer. By asking questions and listening well, both account managers learned of challenges their customer was facing and with which they could help. They learned their accounts' business problems and set up performance-measurement systems. The account managers' assistance resulted in increased sales and, more critically, even deeper account relationships. The customers began seeing the suppliers—U.S. West and 3M—not as vendors but as resources, strategic partners.

CREATE FIRMWIDE RELATIONSHIPS

How can you ensure that your organization is creating firmwide relationships? Ideally, your strategic account manager will:

1. Identify the critical players in the appropriate account buying-influence group(s).

2. Determine the role that each player fills, including:
   • his top three needs;
   • his degree of influence;
   • his preferred communications mode;
   • his desired frequency of contact;
   • his primary supplier contact; and
   • how to deepen the relationship.
3. Use the relationship map checklist to identify gaps in knowledge as well as resources required.
4. Either manage a given buyer-influence relationship or orchestrate another supplier employee's management of the relationship.
5. Set up performance-measurement systems that track back to the goals of the buying influences.
6. Monitor those measurement systems for early warning signs of the customer-loss cycle.
7. Manage the opportunities that then arise.

Key 6: Regularly Quantify and Communicate the Value Received from and Delivered to Strategic Accounts

To succeed as a business strategy, strategic account management requires solid returns from its program and its targeted customer investments—quarter-to-quarter and longer term. The program's executive sponsors and those serving the customer, perhaps working with the finance people, will ideally determine the customer's long-term relationship-asset value and its replacement cost. Knowing these numbers, an executive can decide whether a given investment in the relationship is justified. Conversely, others serving the customer will also quantify the value they deliver to those accounts. Without continually quantifying and communicating that value, there is little way to justify premium prices.

> **Without continually quantifying and communicating that value (delivered to accounts), there is little way to justify premium prices.**

We will be discussing two topics:

1. Quantify the value strategic accounts provided.
2. Quantify the value delivered to strategic accounts.

One of the battles that strategic account management has had to continually fight is the charge that it is based primarily on relationship management, which many often see as a "soft" issue. In several decades of work, we've seen that relationship management is a detailed performance issue requiring a strategic account manager with superior interpersonal and business skills and a firm that has dealt substantively with the seven keys in this book. The firms most effective at strategic account management realize that, if they cannot make a financial case—internally and externally—for the value a given strategic account provides and receives, it makes no sense to invest in that relationship. We've spoken about the importance of portfolio analyses prior to naming an account strategic, but suppliers should also reassess resource allocation to strategic accounts regularly in the light of revenue/profit/costs generated.

Strategic account management, unfortunately, does not easily lend itself to traditional ROI measures, which most executives expect. With estimated payback figures, executives justifiably find it difficult to determine whether a given relationship really merits an investment. Throw in the ever-present need for cost control, and you have created the perfect scenario for firms thinking short-term and underinvesting in customers on whose future they depend.

QUANTIFY THE VALUE STRATEGIC ACCOUNTS PROVIDE

We know a strategic account manager at a design-and-build firm who started a relationship with a division of a global service organization. The account manager started slowly, developing trust with the global facilities manager, and soon signed contracts for three continents, making the services organization one of the design-and-build firm's top three customers. Then the design-and-build firm reorganized and named a field general manager to head its strategic account management program. The field general manager did not really understand what strategic account management was and clung to the management style that had given him success in the field—a focus on strict cost controls.

The SAM began to feel constricted almost immediately. As one example, the services organization needed to custom build part of a facility, which required the design-and-build firm to hire out $1,000 of extra architectural design work. The account manager simply passed the bill to his new boss, seeing it as a justified expense in an account potentially worth hundreds of millions of dollars annually. The new director did not see it that way and said that, if the expense was not specified in the contract, the client would have to pay it, regardless of the account revenue potential. The SAM spent $1,000 of his own money to keep from damaging the relationship—and he began to update his resume. He could see that he was not going to be able to maintain loyal and profitable customer relationships.

Let's see what can be at stake with a strategic account by doing a simple exercise that requires some hard analysis (Figure 7–1).

Calculate the lifetime customer value by following the instructions below:

In Column A, place the name of your top three strategic accounts, defining the top three by whatever your strategic goals are.

In Column B, grade each of those relationships from A for excellent to F for failing.

In Column C, write the annual revenue that each customer generates.

Multiply those totals times 10 for 10 years (Column D) and write the new numbers in Column E. We have used 10 years arbitrarily here. If your relationships tend to last longer, multiply the totals times more years.

In Column F, write the estimated margin percentage on those relationships and multiply them times the dollars times years to calculate the bottom line. The margin number tends to be the figure that people have most trouble coming up with. If your program is up and running, you can come up with a margin percentage by starting with your firm's average gross margin percentage. Then you could adjust it for strategic account management. See Figure 7–2 for adjustment factors.

FIGURE 7-1

Lifetime Customer Exercise

A Account	B	C Annual Sales	D Years	E 10-Year Revenue	F Profit Margin %	G Lifetime Value
		$	× 10 years =	$		
		$	× 10 years =	$		
		$	× 10 years =	$		

F I G U R E   7 – 2

Margin Adjustment Factors

To Decrease SAM Margins	To Increase SAM Margins
Volume discounts	Longer relationships—lower acquisition cost
Co-investment	More opportunity to share in value created
Extra resources required	Introduction to a new market Higher volume = more effectively utilized equipment

If you can come up with a margin percentage, multiply that percentage times the 10-year revenue figures to get the bottom-line value of the relationship over 10 years. If you are not comfortable estimating the margin percentage, use the 10-year revenue figure. We will show a little later how Boise Office Solutions successfully nailed down the margins of its national accounts.

You now have three numbers. Answer the following questions regarding those numbers:

1. Examine the total lifetime values you've computed for your top three accounts. What annual dollar-level value are you currently delivering to each of these customers? How do you know? How does that annual dollar level compare with the value they deliver to you?

   This question jumps us into the second part of this chapter, where some effective firms demonstrate how they quantify value they deliver. For now, if your firm is not quantifying its delivered value, the odds are very good that the customer will neither recognize your value nor see much reason to remain loyal.

2. If you were to lose these three customers, how much would it cost you to develop new account relationships that would generate the same level of revenue or profit? In other words, what are these customers' asset-replacement costs? Would you be able to replace these three customers with three other accounts?

   This is one of those questions that can pale the face of even the most secure executive. No one wants to think about losing a huge customer. Even though businesspeople know that losing such customers means sacrificing a predictable revenue stream over time, it's usually eye opening to see these numbers written in cold, hard print.

   It's as sobering to consider losing these customers as it is to determine exactly what it would cost to replace them. In our experience, few firms have guidelines about what they would spend to replace a major relationship. We do know engineering firms that budget 5 to 10 percent of their annual revenue for special marketing and/or sales expenses; some of these firms apply that 5 to 10 percent as a rule of thumb for acquisition costs. If the customer is worth $10 million annually, the firm is willing to invest $500,000 to $1 million to try to acquire it.

   The reason for the final question regarding the three customers is that, when executives start to think about this issue, they may see that there are not three huge accounts out there "dying to be sold by us," in the words of one executive. In many cases, the firm would have to sell six to nine smaller customers to produce the same level of revenue as the top three generate. Multiplying the number of customers you need to acquire substantially increases the acquisition costs. Next to margin percentage, this is probably the most challenging question in this exercise, but to receive the full benefits of this exercise, you must determine or estimate asset-replacement costs.

3. How much are you currently investing in these relationships to ensure that you don't lose them?

   After working through the previous question, many executives immediately answer this question by saying, "not enough." And that answer tends to get validated when they determine how much they are already investing. Executives usually answer this question by prorating the salaries of the strategic account manager and support people by how much time they dedicate to the account. If you have already gone though the six-question account portfolio exercise in Chapter 4, you may already have the numbers regarding any extraordinary support expenses these accounts have generated.

4. What grades did you assign to these three relationships?

   Be watchful for a grade of C or lower. A C grade is a neutral score—while the account has no particular reason to leave you, neither does it have any particular reason to stay. We consider a C grade as a supplier perched at the edge of the strategic account loss cycle, waiting for a push.

5. What additional investments should you make to ensure the loyalty of these relationships?

   We've noticed that a good SAM (as well as dedicated customer service people) can usually answer this question with specificity and that there is usually a high correlation between the account manager's answer and the answers of critical account contacts. In some cases, the SAM has already been trying to justify these investments over time, but when the supplier quantifies the relationships' lifetime values and replacement costs, the required investments can suddenly take on a new level of urgency.

This exercise lacks the hard-dollar specificity you would find in an ROI case for buying a bulldozer. On the other hand, the relationship asset can easily be thousands of times more valuable than a bulldozer to the supplier over time. This exercise can be a wake-up call to executives who may be thinking short term regarding a long-term asset. It also points to a critical responsibility of the SAM—to continually communicate the value of the account to the supplier. The account is not the only one that has a short memory when value is not regularly quantified.

> . . . [T]he SAM [should] continually communicate the value of the account to the supplier. The account is not the only one that has a short memory when value is not regularly quantified.

For a solid example of quantifying the value of a customer, let's turn to Boise Office Solutions, whose executives were frustrated by their inability to determine the profitability of national accounts. Their solution yielded reliable customer profitability and provided a value-added software package that BOS then offered to those same national accounts to serve their customers.

BOISE OFFICE SOLUTIONS

Boise Office Solutions (BOS), headquartered in Itasca, Illinois, is a controlled subsidiary of Boise Cascade Corporation. In 2001, BOS generated national account sales of $1.6 billion in office supplies, copy paper, computer products, furniture, and advertising specialty items. This is a very impressive number, even allowing for BOS's revenue growth by acquisition. BOS's goal is to provide next-day delivery of its entire range of products in its full-line catalog—at consistent prices and service levels to customers throughout the United States. As national suppliers know, this is not an easy goal to achieve. But BOS has achieved it—for some of its largest domestic customers. Of BOS's 1000+ national accounts, a great many are in the Fortune

500. BOS believes it still has tremendous opportunities for continued growth in the Fortune 500 and just below.

BOS's selection criteria for national accounts are those potential customers who:

- spend at least $250,000 per year on office products (BOS' average national account spends $1 million annually);

- have at least three BOS locations (distribution centers) serving them;

- are creditworthy;

- have a centralized initiative to negotiate a nationwide agreement; and

- have some internal team that will organize the interface with BOS.

Once BOS selected and served multiple national accounts, though, the multiple distribution centers for multiple national account divisions made it very difficult to determine these customers' profitability. As a distributor, BOS is traditionally concerned with the cost of goods in relation to sales and with big buckets of administrative costs. But BOS's parent company, Boise Cascade Corp., is primarily a manufacturing company, paying close attention to cost accounting. As BOS grew dramatically in the early 1990s, Boise Cascade Corp.'s culture influenced BOS to better understand its own costs and to tell if a given national account was profitable or not. The profitability model was also driven by the frustration of BOS's executives, who did not know the true profitability of their national accounts.

As an initial step in understanding its costs, BOS decided to define and study its business processes. BOS identified 78 processes involved in conducting its business at the distribution centers. These include such activities as bin-order pulling, bulk-order pulling, order entry, collection activities, receiving at the distribution centers, shipping from the distribution centers, sales calls, and pricing. Once BOS defined and studied these processes, it used activity-based costing (ABC) methods to compute BOS's overall cost/process.

BOS dispatched ABC teams to its distribution centers to review the frequency of these processes and determine what each one cost. The ABC teams even included in their analyses costs such as forklift depreciation for each process in a distribution center. The activity-based costing team provided BOS with a cost per process per distribution center. BOS could then compute the average cost per process across the whole company—and could standardize the most cost-efficient processes. Once standardized, the distribution centers' processes were easily costed. For example, BOS now (January 2003) knows that it costs $1.06 to enter one stock-keeping unit (SKU) while taking a telephone order and that it costs only 36¢ per SKU if the order arrives via electronic data interchange (EDI). BOS completed this costing analysis for all 78 identified processes.

From this point, it was possible to take the same approach at the customer level. For instance, BOS's mainframe can tell whether a particular order came in through a customer-service telephone call or through EDI. BOS just had to identify which processes it used to serve the national account and then calculate how many times each process was performed on its behalf. The firm also accounted for all overhead costs. Because BOS already had an excellent handle on product gross margin per customer, it just needed to determine a pretax profit figure for each national customer by subtracting the costs to serve it. In the case of a multidivision national account, BOS just rolls up all of the product gross margins, the different locations' process costs to serve, and other overhead figures to calculate the profitability for that customer. As a value-add for strategic accounts, BOS will also generate reports that compare a strategic account's buying habits in New York to its buying habits in Chicago. BOS can also compare the purchasing patterns of different account divisions within a single location.

While BOS was solving its challenge, its national account managers were explaining to national accounts the basis for its process costing. The customers frequently asked, "What's in it for us to change our buying processes?" Thinking that its customers could gain efficiencies similar to those it had achieved, BOS chose to take the skill "to the customer's side." Introducing this analysis to each customer using BOS's ABC teams was, however, not practical (although BOS briefly considered going into the activities-based consulting business). As an alternative, BOS decided to create ABC software so its national accounts could duplicate the process it had gone through.

BOS asked a senior marketing analyst to create the software. Using the assistance of an outside software firm, he was able to document and automate the steps BOS had been taking internally. The end result was a program called "SAVE." BOS developed marketing materials to support the software before the company offered the program to national accounts. BOS also had to train its people how to use the program—sales reps could not rely on the ABC teams when they were working with their customers. In addition, BOS had to teach them basic accounting and activity-based costing concepts. BOS designed a training curriculum with disks, PowerPoint presentations, and hard copies of worksheets for the BOS sales managers. After the sales managers went to Chicago for training, they returned to their offices to train the national account managers and the sales reps.

The "SAVE" program requires the national account to input some basic information concerning its purchasing processes: the number of minutes the particular process takes, the average compensation of people doing the process (including average benefit costs), and some additional variables such as whether they are buying from a catalog or online. This time the program multiplies those factors by the resource costs to get a total cost per process. The software then multiplies the resulting cost per process by the number of times BOS performs the process for them—a figure BOS can access from its mainframe—to provide them with the total costs they pay for using that process over time.

"SAVE" helps BOS national accounts get a clear picture of many processes, including:

- Requisitioning—when an associate requests replacement office products.
- Order placing—when the purchasing department places an order for the office products.

- Receiving and distributing—when the office products arrive at the customer's site.
- Accounts payable—when the customer's accounting department pays the office-products supplier.

Once a BOS customer has learned its total cost for these processes, the BOS SAM offers to do some "what-if" modeling to explore ways to reduce costs. Suggestions may include using EDI instead of the fax machine, managing the billing process electronically, or placing batch orders on certain days of the week. The SAM, at this point in a consultative role, gives the customer a series of options. For each option, he/she can identify an expected savings to the customer.

Purchasing people typically don't get that excited about these soft-dollar cost savings, because their company usually measures their performance based on the price they pay. Finance people, however, have been very impressed with SAVE. The CFOs of some of BOS's national accounts have asked why their other suppliers are not providing the same data to them (always a good sign).

BOS can point to many benefits of the "SAVE" program both for itself and its national accounts. BOS can help the customer save money at the interface between the two firms. Just as valuable, though, is the benefit that "SAVE" can offer the *customers* of BOS's national accounts.

Medicon, a BOS national account, offers an excellent example of how to achieve these benefits. Medicon, a large hospital buying group, is an umbrella organization that contracts with medical-supply providers such as Allegiance Healthcare, which cover many hospitals' needs. The Medicon salespeople call on the hospitals' chief administrators, as opposed to their purchasing departments. Medicon suspected that it could use "SAVE" for products it sells, such as surgical supplies and gowns. The firm has, in fact, used the "SAVE" software to help lower its customers' costs. BOS has elevated the value it brings to its national accounts and, in this case particularly, the value its national accounts bring to *their* customers. It's a natural win-win solution.

And there are other wins. In many cases, actions that national accounts take to save money also save money for BOS. For example, when a customer implements EDI to save money, BOS also saves money in areas such as forms, reduced mistakes resulting from human error, number of days sales are outstanding, and on collection activities.

Helping its national accounts win, both by lowering their purchasing costs and providing value to the national accounts' customers, puts BOS in a position to gain additional share of the national accounts' business. BOS's national accounts now view them not as an office-products company that provides commodities, but also as a provider of business and organizational solutions. Admittedly, this case is based on BOS taking advantage of a relatively unique situation where its own processes involved at the customer interface are generic and reversible with the purchasing processes of its national accounts. At the same time, however, we know of very few suppliers that have captured the costs of their 20/80 processes—the 20 percent of its processes that generate 80 percent of its costs to serve. Determining the costs of those processes and using them to determine customer profitability would in most cases be a major improvement. And activities-based costing, the discipline required to do such accounting, has been around for decades.

QUANTIFY THE VALUE DELIVERED TO STRATEGIC ACCOUNTS

The ABC principles behind "SAVE" make it an effective tool that most strategic account management programs could use. It provides better customer profitability, and it offers solid value for the accounts the supplier serves. The other half of the value equation, though, is to quantify the value *delivered* to customers. To cover that topic, let's examine two firms whose means for quantifying value to customers are as effective as they are creative. Let's first look at Holland Hitch.

THE HOLLAND HITCH STORY

Holland Hitch, a 75-year-old family-owned business head-quartered in Holland, Michigan, manufactures premium-quality truck and trailer components throughout the U.S., Europe, and the Far East. Holland sells to three primary customers: trailer OEMs, tractor OEMs, and large fleet owners. In the mid-nineties, Holland saw that almost half of its total available opportunity was in the large-fleet segment, a niche in which Holland had historically been least successful. Fleet buyers tend to focus intensely on purchase price and so were unwilling to buy Holland's premium-priced components. Holland knew that, if it wanted to continue growing, it would have to develop a strategy to penetrate the large fleets.

In 1996, Holland promoted Dan Millar, who had successfully sold Holland products to large fleets, to become its manager of national accounts. Holland asked that Millar develop a national account management program to serve the large-fleet segment. After the promotion, Millar considered how Holland might sell differently to large-fleet buyers. In his own selling, Millar regularly quantified value. As an example, Holland sells a fifth wheel—the large metal wheel that attaches the truck to the trailer. Holland's fifth wheel had a premium price, but it was made of aluminum, which meant it was lighter than the steel fifth wheels that competitors manufactured. Millar determined how much gasoline the lighter Holland fifth wheel saved a tractor trailer during a year and showed that its gas savings more than made up for the price differential. He then did the same for Holland's two other major components: suspensions (mechanical and air) and landing gears. He put the numbers on a spreadsheet and started to sell using that spreadsheet.

While calling on a fleet buyer's office, Millar would start by asking what sorts of components the Fleet would be looking to buy or replace that year. These always included items from Holland's product mix. Then Millar would explain the value that each Holland component offered one tractor-trailer, entering them on the spreadsheet. The spreadsheet instantly added the savings for one tractor-trailer. The sales closer for Millar often came when he asked how many tractor-trailers the account had in its fleet. When he entered that number, the spreadsheet would multiply savings times total tractor-trailers. Many times, the number was in the hundreds of thousands of dollars. The sale at that point was not assured, but quantifying Holland's total value versus what his competitors were offering guaranteed that Holland would be considered very carefully. And the sales numbers started growing dramatically.

The spreadsheet eventually became too cumbersome, and Holland funded the development of a relational database that Millar had envisioned, called Component Value Analysis (CVA). CVA continued to quantify component value, but also captured fleet operational data and cost drivers. After the Holland account managers had entered a baseline amount of performance data, the CVA became a performance indicator. It could tell fleet buyers exactly where they were spending too much money in certain areas—such as oil or maintenance, for example. Holland's normative performance database allowed it to offer a value that its competitors could not.

Holland's final success? After developing CVA, hiring new people, and training its field sales representatives how to become national account managers, Holland generated more than $50 million in incremental revenue from 1996-2000. Holland's president declared that the national account program was the single most effective marketing initiative in the company's history. Perhaps most important, Holland's use of CVA with its customers has been the starting point of a major restructuring of its overall marketing strategy. The software shows the importance of viewing product value from the customer's perspective and has resulted in an increased sense of customer responsiveness from all parts of Holland Hitch, from marketing to engineering to manufacturing. All this came about because a gifted national account manager started quantifying the value that Holland delivered to a targeted segment.

The Holland case is interesting because the CVA program, designed to quantify customer value, became the focal point of the organization becoming aligned to serve the customer. Our third case shows another creative national account manager,

Rich Mistkowski, and how he was able to recover and expand orders from a customer that had booted out his company, National Office Supplies, for delivering no value.

THE NATIONAL OFFICE SUPPLIES STORY

In 1991, National Office Supplies (now a part of Staples), a $125 million business headquartered in Hackensack, New Jersey, lost one of its largest customers, Countrywide Funding, based in Pasadena, California. Countrywide, then the largest domestic home mortgage and lending firm, was benefiting hugely from prevailing low interest rates at the time. Its growth was explosive—it was adding 20 branches every two to three months. More critically to National, though, Countrywide was a $600,000-a-year customer—or rather, an ex-customer.

According to Rich Mistkowski, whom National brought in as national account manager to recover the customer, National lost Countrywide because it was managing the account "by assumption." For instance, National had assumed that longevity equaled loyalty. That assumption led National down a reactive path in service quality and in relationship management. The prior account manager sold—or rather wrote orders from—one person in procurement. He had not bothered to analyze Countrywide's purchasing practices to see if National could offer it a competitive and compelling value equation. Neither had he developed metrics to measure National's performance at Countrywide. As a result, neither the account manager nor National really understood what was at stake—until Countrywide's VP of procurement, a volatile individual, noted little value in the National relationship and booted it out.

In October 1991, Mistkowski moved to southern California and started to analyze Countrywide's office-supplies procurement processes. He found that Countrywide, which at that point had 104 regional branches, was buying all of its office supplies, computer supplies, and copier supplies from a local California supplier, which in turn was shipping those supplies to each of the offices via UPS.

Mistkowski made some assumptions (which turned out to be conservative) and started totaling these costs. He assumed that in a given two-month period, each Countrywide branch was sending 26 orders at $100 each to its office-supplies vendor. Each of these orders cost $50 to ship UPS second day. This meant that in any two months, Countrywide was spending $135,000 on shipping and $270,000 on product. Annually that came to $1,620,000 in shipping and $3,240,000 in product costs. Mistkowski also determined that many Countrywide branches, unhappy with the corporate vendor's service levels, were buying office supplies locally and paying retail prices. At the same time, Countrywide was incurring huge billing-processing costs because the vendor was sending each branch an individual bill for each order—using Mistkowski's assumptions, a total of 156 bills per branch per year.

These cost figures were excellent news for National because its distribution system and bulk purchasing could help save Countrywide a bundle. Mistkowski determined that National's Los Angeles office alone could supply 89 percent of all Countrywide branches' office-supply needs—within 24 hours and with no additional shipping charges. It could supply the remaining 11 percent within 48 hours, again with no shipping charges. Throw in National's other distribution centers—in Chicago, Atlanta, Dallas (where National had seven distribution centers), Baltimore, Boston, and New Jersey—and National could immediately cut Countrywide's annual office-supply freight expenses by $1.6 million and, in the process, give better service and product prices. Unlike Countrywide's vendor, National bought in bulk and therefore received an additional 35 percent discount, some of which it would pass on to Countrywide. This was an opportunity that account managers dream about.

After he had presented his business case for recovering the Countrywide relationship to National executives, Mistkowski started to develop multiple relationships at Countrywide to understand Countrywide's business and the members of the buying group to whom he could best present National's value equation. Mistkowski could see that, with its explosive growth, Countrywide was not much focused on savings, but he could also see that Countrywide really didn't understand how much it was overspending on office supplies.

In April 1992, Mistkowski got his toe in the Countrywide door when it awarded National its Xerox toner and cartridge business, worth more than $1.7 million to National. This time, National took nothing for granted regarding the Countrywide relationship. Mistkowski formed an internal Countrywide team at National, composed of the regional VP to whom he reported, National's president, a customer-service specialist, and three other employees from the National Customer Service Team. In August 1992, the National-Countrywide team began scheduling monthly meetings at which National quantified all savings Countrywide was reaping by doing business with National, National's performance (percent fill rates, etc.), and any service problems that had emerged and how quickly they had been solved. National also instituted EDI billing, which it estimated created an additional minimum 10 percent savings in Countrywide's procurement costs.

Another landmark event occurred in August 1992, when Mistkowski finally established a relationship with an executive who could simply say "yes" to making National a sole-source vendor for Countrywide's office supplies. Countrywide had initiated a total-quality initiative, and its VP of quality assurance was looking for ways to improve service and lower costs. Mistkowski laid out the financial case he had developed almost nine months earlier, demonstrated savings in the existing toner and cartridge business, and finally heard the question he had been waiting for—the VP of quality assurance asked why National wasn't supplying *all* of Countrywide's office products. Mistkowski said he'd love to do that (he'd been drafting a proposal for months). Countrywide crafted an RFP that was almost custom-tailored to National's capabilities. In October 1992, National won the business. A lost customer worth $600,000 a year suddenly returned to National as a five-year sole-source contract worth $5.5 million a year.

As part of this contract, Countrywide established a shared-savings program in which, if an item's former cost was

$10 and National could supply the same item at a 10 percent discount, Countrywide shared the savings with National by paying $9.50 for the item. This shared-savings plan was to continue, with a notable exception, described below.

In strategic account relationships, very little remains stable. In December 1993, Countrywide's VP of procurement (the volatile person who originally ended the National relationship) was replaced by an executive whom Countrywide charged with removing $300,000 from its office-supplies purchasing costs. Mistkowski and his team decided to think long term and make a large investment in the Countrywide relationship.

Mistkowski went to the new VP of procurement and laid out a plan that would allow Countrywide to save not just $300,000, but $650,000+ during the next 12 months. First, Mistkowski showed that Countrywide was currently buying OEM office products, such as an IBM cartridge, for $200 each. A remanufactured cartridge with the same specs, on the other hand, cost only $125. Because the cartridges were Countrywide's number-one purchased item, a switch to remanufactured parts meant saving $450,000 a year in cartridge costs alone. Several other OEM parts could be replaced with remanufactured parts for an additional $200,000 in savings a year. In an hour's presentation, Mistkowski provided the means by which the new VP of procurement could exceed his savings targets and make his bonus. National gave up some revenue and margin, but Mistkowski believed this was an investment in the overall relationship, which, given Countrywide's still booming growth (it now had 450 locations), National would recoup. And he was correct. By quantifying both Countrywide's value to National and National's value to Countrywide, Mistkowski had transformed a former account into one of National's largest customers.

National Office Supplies didn't really think about Countrywide's lifetime value until it was booted out. Only then did National ask hard questions and make critical investments in recovering the Countrywide relationship. It assigned a national account manager to Countrywide and had the patience to let that account manager do his job. That job included quantifying the value that National provided to Countrywide. When National saw the results—an account moving from $600,000 to $0 to $5.5 million a year—it decided to redesign its national account management program using Mistkowki's approach.

Firms that do quantify the value they receive from and deliver to customers tend to be more successful in their strategic account management.

We are now regularly seeing accounts that require their suppliers to quantify the value they deliver—sometimes when the customer itself does not quantify value delivered to its customers. At the same time, more supplier executives want a detailed reporting of the value, both of strategic accounts and the account management program.

Firms that do quantify the value they receive from and deliver to customers tend to be more successful in their strategic account management. BOS, Holland, and National were each able to take away share from their competitors because no one else in their industry had differentiated on quantified value. Value quantification remains a strategy that can differentiate a supplier's offerings to strategic accounts. One of the very best strategic account managers we know, when asked what his job was, replied, "I deliver value to my customers and my company. I regularly tell both what that value is and then I tell them again and then, just for a change of pace, I tell them again. Unless it is quantified, value doesn't exist."

REGULARLY QUANTIFY AND COMMUNICATE THE VALUE RECEIVED FROM AND DELIVERED TO STRATEGIC ACCOUNTS

How can you ensure that you are regularly quantifying the value you receive from and deliver to strategic accounts?

1. Go through the lifetime customer exercise, initially with your three most critical accounts.

2. Take a hard look at the value you deliver to those accounts, their replacement costs, and what investments your people believe your company needs to make in those relationships.

3. During this exercise, if you question your profitability data, meet with the departments that have cost data and develop a profitability model to calculate what numbers really matter to them.

4. Calculate the cost of your processes. Your firm probably won't be able to do it as completely as BOS, but it can certainly focus on 20 percent of the processes that generate 80 percent of its costs.

5. Then, if you do not currently quantify value you deliver to clients, develop a means for doing so. Isolate the value of products from the value of services you deliver. As we saw with both BOS and Holland, a piece of software that automates this process can be very effective.

6. If you have industry or customer-performance data, compare for the account what it costs for it to do the business with what it costs you to do the business (assuming your process has greater efficiency and effectiveness than the customer's). Given the size of your critical customers, you may be able to make a case to do some activities-based costing at their firms and yours.

7. If possible, develop a normative performance database (as Holland did) with your clients to determine where their costs are too high.

8. If the value is very difficult to quantify, work with your strategic account. When you explain that you want to quantify the value it is receiving, the account usually will help you define that value.

CHAPTER 8

Key 7: Use Technology Judiciously

We need to be clear: we have seen technology serve as an invaluable tool for firms managing large numbers of customers. We have also invested significant amounts to automate what we believe should be automated in our companies. It's an astonishingly creative time for business computer applications—firms are developing new applications almost weekly to assist in relationship management, professional development, and collaboration.

At the same time, though, we notice a disturbing trend. Firms in too many cases assume that technology is the best way to solve their problems, so they invest in systems when there might be better solutions. Given the financial and human resources that technology can consume, the decision whether or not a firm should invest in systems should be exceedingly rigorous and should factor in alternative tools or nontechnology solutions.

In this chapter we will examine two topics:

1. A high-level overview of Customer Relationship Management (CRM) systems challenges.
2. The seven steps to successful systems implementation for strategic account management programs.

A HIGH-LEVEL OVERVIEW OF CRM SYSTEMS CHALLENGES

At a certain point in the life of a strategic account management program, a need arises that may indicate a technological solution—internal or external communication, collaboration, contact management, or account planning, for example. Whatever the need is, it drives a potentially dangerous choice point. The question firms face at this point is, "Should we invest in technology?" The choice can be dangerous because the costs of some customer relationship management (CRM) and sales-force automation systems easily run into the millions of dollars, and may require millions more if problems arise (as they often do) in the system's implementation.

In our experience, there is a further challenge for strategic account management programs: most companies implement CRM systems primarily for their nonstrategic salesforces: field sales, telemarketers, perhaps customer service people. This means that adapting or reconfiguring the CRM software to meet the needs of the strategic account management program is often an afterthought. If the CRM system has been designed primarily to serve the firm's other and larger salesforces, the system's strategic account management capabilities may be cumbersome add-ons, making it difficult for the account managers to integrate the system into the way they work.

> . . . [B]eing technology-driven can be a very expensive bandwagon for the supplier to hop on.

Let's start with a high-level distinction a colleague once made between "technology-driven" and "technology-supported" companies. The technology-driven company, too often before determining its strategic and user needs, invests in the "latest and greatest" technological breakthrough. Given the costs of these systems, though, being technology-driven can be a very expensive bandwagon for the supplier to hop on.

The technology-supported company, on the other hand, determines its needs, strategic and operational, and then finds the best tools—not necessarily computerized—to support those needs.

One technology-driven manufacturing firm invested in Enterprise Resource Planning (ERP) software in the late 1980s because the software sellers led them to believe the software offered a "total solution." After spending millions of dollars on the package, the company had a nightmarish and unfinished implementation. When many manufacturing employees complained about how time-consuming the system was to use, the firm asked the long-gone sellers for help. The sellers said they would be happy to help customize and re-implement the ERP software—for several more million dollars. Those who had bought the software did not want to admit they had made a bad decision, so the firm invested once again to get the assistance. The firm re-implemented the ERP system with training and support and waited for all its problems to disappear. After six months, though, the firm's IT department did a systems audit and found less than 30 percent of the organization using the ERP software, even though the firm had mandated its use. It took more than three years before the system started to truly help the firm. No one wanted to estimate how many man-years of productivity had been lost getting the ERP system up and running.

Ignoring the needs of strategic account managers can effectively negate whatever increased productivity the system offers.

We bring up ERP software because the push for CRM software offered a parallel situation—at least up to 2001, when the CRM boom slowed considerably. During the CRM sales cycle, most buyers heard "total solution" (which to us is the equivalent of promising the paperless office) over and over, as CRM sellers promised the software offered large numbers and kinds of features. And, in our experience, it was the rare vendor who, when asked if her software would handle a given problem, would admit that her program could not. The larger CRM systems tend to be very expensive—in the millions—and their implementation tends to be rough and sometimes more expensive. Too often CRM system purchasers haven't thoroughly determined what support their strategic account managers really required, particularly when, as usually happens, these CRM systems focus on field sales or telesales. Sometimes the best a VP of strategic accounts can hope for is to be on the committee that determines what functionality the CRM system will have. But the VP of strategic accounts still has only one vote. Ignoring the needs of strategic account managers can effectively negate whatever increased productivity the system offers.

As one strategic account manager told us, "It's not like I have a lot of free time to sit around, typing account plans and populating databases . . . and they never asked me what I needed."

In our experience, the system's implementation always takes far longer than vendors suggest, and even then it can be easier to get the system up and running than it is to get the account managers to use the program. They may have a compelling reason. The role of a strategic account manager—or that of any strategic account seller—requires huge time-management challenges. Given the numbers of customers and individual relationships most strategic account managers oversee, it is the rare account manager who will allow anything not immediately helpful to eat her time. As one strategic account manager told us, "It's not like I have a lot of free time to sit around, typing account plans and populating databases . . . and they never asked me what I needed."

Over time we have seen many successful and unsuccessful CRM/salesforce automation implementations. We'd like to share seven high-level steps that successful firms—and strategic account program directors—tend to take. Then comes the case of UPS, which succeeded in dramatically improving communications with an internally designed system targeted at its national account managers.

SEVEN STEPS TO SUCCESSFUL SYSTEMS IMPLEMENTATION FOR STRATEGIC ACCOUNT MANAGEMENT PROGRAMS

FIGURE 8–1

Seven Steps to Successful Systems Implementation

Step One: Identify critical strategic account management performance needs within the context of the sales and account management processes.

Step Two: Identify and speak to noncompetitive firms that have successfully implemented technology solutions for their strategic account management programs.

Step Three: Filter—which of the identified strategic account management performance needs identified in step one could best be met by technology?

Step Four: Assess the technology-readiness of both the strategic account managers and anyone else who will be using the system.

Step Five: Develop and support tech-based solutions.

Step Six: Implementation-pilot, then rollout.

Step Seven: Review and revise tools.

Step One: identify critical strategic account management performance needs within the context of the sales and account management processes.

To determine the best tools for the job, it is critical that your firm conduct a thorough needs analysis, working through its sales and account management processes to determine performance needs of the strategic account management group. This needs analysis must also provide a list of how account management team members are currently meeting those needs. This is hands-down the best place to start, although, in our experience, it is not a common starting place. A surprising number of firms assume they already know what their strategic account management team members could use. Time and again, though, we have seen that, if the CRM system does not speak directly to their needs, strategic account team members will ignore their laptops or do just enough work on the system to keep management off their backs. This is not irresponsibility on their part; indeed, assuming the system really doesn't help, it is the height of responsibility.

Getting the strategic account team members' buy-in for any sort of automation that impacts them is as important as getting cross-functional buy-in for the strategic account management program. We said earlier that the best a VP of strategic accounts can sometimes hope for is to serve on the committee that selects the CRM system and its functional uses. We strongly suggest that the VP of strategic Accounts lobby for this position because if there is no one on the committee speaking for strategic accounts, only luck will allow strategic account managers and their team members to get anything they need. Whoever does the CRM needs analysis must be able to listen carefully to what the account management people say they need and then translate those needs into tools.

Step Two: Identify and speak to noncompetitive firms that have successfully implemented technology solutions for their strategic account management programs.

You can usually learn a great deal about implementing CRM and other strategic account management tools by speaking to those who have already done it. Ask your vendors for the names of firms that have successfully implemented their product and then do your own search for other noncompetitive firms on the Internet, at conferences, and in print. Look for firms that have a salesforce similar to yours. Ask those firms what they would do differently if they were to implement such tools again and, ideally, how they handled some of your company's needs. Six weeks of research here can save years of lost opportunity costs.

Step Three: Filter—which of the identified strategic account management performance needs identified in step one could best be met by technology?

Here is a step too often left out. When systems people conduct a needs analysis, they tend to see automation as a solution, even when it is inappropriate. Automation is what IT folks do. In too many systems implementations, bad processes get automated, which results in employees making bad decisions that much faster. At the same time, a CRM system cannot help with performance needs caused by poor compensation design, lack of training, or unrealistic account assignments, all challenges previously mentioned.

Someone—usually outside the IT department—needs to ask questions carefully about where to spend system-development dollars. In too many cases, IT folks, unable to downshift their technical vocabulary, smack into sales executives who have a limited tolerance for techno-babble, and the critical filter question can get answered by the IT people alone. When that happens, strategic account managers can find themselves hampered by a system that was supposed to help them. We recall one firm, hip-deep in putting together design specifications for its CRM system, which could see that the system was not going to meet some of the most critical strategic account manager needs. The firm's VP of strategic accounts then bought business intelligence software, which allowed the account managers to pull data and generate reports from most of the firm's other systems. To the strategic account managers, these were the most critical needs.

Step Four: Assess the technology-readiness of both the strategic account managers and anyone else who will be using the system.

In too many cases, systems developers tend to treat system users as the single most flexible part of the system, an error that can—and usually does—have huge negative repercussions. An employee with no past experience with technology, who is uncomfortable with computers, or who finds it very difficult to change work habits, will not view a new system with delight.

Training and documentation . . . are rungs, which, left out of the implementation ladder, can lead to a nasty fall.

Seldom have we seen systems developers conduct any sort of technology-readiness assessment to determine how comfortable the targeted users are with automation. This kind of assessment should answer questions such as: How technology-savvy are the system's potential users? How technology-savvy is the firm within which the system will operate? How technology-ready are the strategic account managers? If your firm's account managers are all middle-aged and depend on their children to help them with computers (as does one of our authors), they will need hands-on training when the company rolls out the system. We know a consultant who spent years helping organizations write, evaluate, and analyze requests for proposals regarding systems implementations. He told us that he never saw a proposal for a system implementation that hadn't underestimated the time the process would take and that hadn't underfunded the training and documentation side of the implementation. These are rungs, which, left out of the implementation ladder, can lead to a nasty fall.

Step Five: Develop and support tech-based solutions.

So far, the firm in our example has identified the critical performance issues, identified which of those issues technology can best solve, and determined the technological-readiness of the targeted users. Now it is time to develop the tech-based solutions. Such solutions may or may not be part of a CRM system, but all relate back to the firm's and users' needs. Lately we have seen collaborative web-based Internet tools that allow SAMs to collaborate in ways never before possible. Sophisticated databases can also track and mine massive amounts of relationship information. And firms—such as Holland Hitch and Boise Office Solutions—use that data to create performance baselines for their customers, developing a competitive advantage in the process. Without having gone through those first three steps, though, resources could easily be diverted to develop solutions that should not be tech-based or that might be very different if the user's computer readiness had been considered.

Unless strategic account management is vigorous in defending its needs, CRM solutions will typically be geared at the firm's larger sales forces.

The role of strategic account leadership here is to make sure their firm applies resources to some of the tools required by account managers. Recall our earlier suggestion: executives in strategic account management programs should attend and participate in systems project-review meetings to make sure that the people purchasing and developing the technology address their needs. As we've said, unless strategic account management is vigorous in defending its needs, CRM solutions will typically be geared at the firm's larger salesforces.

Second, we suggest that directors not wait until the end of systems development to state needs or make requests. The further along the systems-development process is, the more expensive it is to make changes. Systems people may sometimes be difficult to interact with, but it will be much more difficult for strategic account managers to work with a system whose design had little or no input from them.

. . . a firm that fails to invest in training and support for systems will pay for the lack of them.

To support those solutions, a firm that fails to invest in training and support for systems will pay for the lack of them. Hidden costs are costs nonetheless.

These paragraphs could be the thesis for another book. It's enough to say that there are many sources about developing and supporting tech-based solutions.

Step Six: Implementation—pilot, then rollout.

Sadly, many systems implementations, after a study of system-design specifications, start here, and many even skip the pilot. When this happens, the SAM suddenly finds himself with a program that has been thrust upon him. Is it any wonder that strategic account managers have sometimes resisted technology?

Getting the strategic account managers' blessing is critical when a system offers them solutions. It seems obvious, but very few firms conduct these sorts of needs and technology-readiness assessments. Nor have they implemented systems in waves—setting up pilots that generate system improvements before full rollout. Ideally, a firm might take a small cross-section of SAMs and team members to help identify the system's kinks. It's much easier to deal with system problems before many people start using it.

Step Seven: Review and revise tools.

Once the firm rolls out the system to all users, it needs to systematically collect user feedback to make changes on an ongoing basis. Few things are more dispiriting than facing a system that makes the same mistake day after day. If users are not technology-oriented, they may blame themselves for the errors, which can lead to much lengthier and more expensive implementations.

These are the seven steps we have seen organizations take in successful systems implementations. They are certainly not the only way to have such success, but they provide a picture many firms lack when they invest in systems.

Let's examine an excellent example of a firm that successfully implemented a communication system to support strategic account management—UPS and its LINK program.

THE UPS STORY: THE DEVELOPMENT OF THE LINK SYSTEM

United Parcel Service (UPS) is a 100-year-old company with more than 300,000 employees serving 200+ countries. Its revenues total $20+ billion, and it is recognized as the world's largest shipping company. In the late 1980s, the UPS salespeople were customer service reps. When the shipping industry deregulated, UPS was forced to develop a sales organization to proactively market its services. Initially, UPS' salesforce was organized along product and geographic lines (UPS' internal processing needs), but in 1993 the company deployed its salesforce based on customer needs. In 1996, UPS redesigned its sales organization to serve three different types of customers:

1. National accounts—customers expected to purchase $1 million a year or more of UPS services.
2. Major accounts—customers expected to purchase $250,000 to $1 million a year UPS services.
3. Key accounts—customers expected to purchase less than $250,000 a year of UPS services but requiring special attention.

UPS employs a two-tiered approach to working with national accounts. UPS National Account Managers (NAMs) create and coordinate corporate-level initiatives with each of their national customers. These NAMs have offices in or near the national customer headquarters and interact with corporate decision makers. UPS National Account Executives (NAEs) work in the field, executing any corporate-level agreements at individual shipping locations. At those locations, NAEs typically communicate the services UPS agreed to provide and help facilitate the delivery of those services. Because UPS' national accounts have been very clear in their expectation that UPS would provide consistent service at all their shipping locations, communication between the NAMs and the NAEs is crucial to success.

And here lay UPS' challenge: communication among UPS corporate, the NAMs, and the NAEs was done through traditional means—written memos, faxes, next-day document shipments, and exchanging voice messages. This didn't work very effectively for several reasons. First, because the specificity and amount of information being shared, which was huge. Second, while UPS makes service commitments to its national customers, most of these accounts do not, in turn, dictate mandatory practices to individual customer shipping locations. This means that different locations would have different expectations regarding service. UPS realized that only a very efficient means of communication could overcome both those barriers. UPS further believed that, if they did it right, such an improvement would ultimately translate into a competitive advantage.

Starting with the clearly defined need to communicate more effectively regarding its national account agreements, UPS started planning the development of what became known as the LINK system, which involved three initial steps:

1. UPS looked at other companies with salesforces comparable to that of UPS and that had been successful in developing and using automated sales-force communications systems.
2. UPS then researched existing commercially available software programs that could meet UPS' needs.

3. UPS enlisted the services of a consulting firm to guide the design of the automated communication system.

Then UPS assessed in detail what capabilities corporate, NAMs, and NAEs believed the system needed to provide. The internal developers decided that the following tools needed to be included:

- contact management software;
- e-mail capabilities; and
- word processing, spreadsheet, database, and presentation package 'office suite' software.

Beyond these basic needs, UPS and its national account team wanted the LINK system to facilitate the communication to implement UPS national account contracts quickly and consistently.

Once UPS identified its system requirements, it drew upon both external and internal resources to build the system. A software-consulting firm designed the "front end"—the laptop computers NAMs and NAEs used. This package included a combination of off-the-shelf and customized software designed to meet the requirements of system users. UPS internally developed the resident database, or "back end" of the system, which stores the information accessed by the laptops. UPS first piloted the LINK system with NAMs, gathering feedback to improve the system, and later rolled it out to all NAEs.

Primarily, though, the LINK system provided a powerful communications tool for implementing national account contracts. LINK allowed NAEs to determine precisely the commitments made by both UPS and the national account at the corporate level. NAEs are then able to work with individual shipping locations to sell and implement these service features.

LINK benefits customers in two major ways: consistency of service and speed. Before the LINK system, UPS found that implementation of national account contracts required 45 to 60 days—mostly because of the problems with traditional communication. Since LINK has been in place, national contracts could be implemented in 14 days on average—a reduction from two months to two weeks.

UPS' major benefits in using the LINK system include:

Efficiency of the national account salesforce. LINK virtually eliminated paperwork hassles and it significantly reduced the time required to communicate effectively among the NAMs and the various national account shipping locations.

Provides NAMs with strategic information. The system allows NAMs to collect information from all NAEs serving national account shipping locations. This information plays a major role in developing national account business plans. LINK thus provides NAMs with an invaluable stream of information for creating customer management strategies.

Allows NAMs to evaluate the effectiveness of business plans. Information captured through LINK not only supports development of national account business plans, it allows UPS to monitor more easily whether it is meeting or exceeding the goals in these plans. If goals are not being met, LINK can help to identify where changes are necessary.

Allows UPS to know exactly what is going on with the customer. By reviewing account information and account history maintained in the LINK system, UPS personnel can instantly identify the national account decision makers and can assess the status of the relationship.

Since we wrote this case in 1997, UPS has developed several new components of LINK—both an intranet and an Internet capability. The intranet leads to greater collaboration among those who work on national accounts, and the Internet allows NAMs to conduct secondary research on customers and industries.

UPS provides an excellent example of a firm approaching technology judiciously. That was one of its keys to success. UPS is clearly a technology-supported organization that went through most of the seven implementation steps outlined above. It first carefully determined a major performance problem—the efficient execution of national agreements. UPS then broke down that performance problem into its components and asked what parts could be solved by a technical solution. It researched other firms and their technology solutions. It then developed tech-based solutions for those problems where appropriate. UPS' LINK implementation was incremental, starting with some NAMs. After they ironed out the system's kinks, the company rolled out LINK to the NAEs and corporate. And system users' feedback guided improvements and system growth. Only when the users' additional needs became clear did UPS add more functionality to LINK. It's an excellent example of a very thoughtful firm succeeding where so many firms have failed.

USE TECHNOLOGY JUDICIOUSLY

How can your firm judiciously harness technology for strategic account management?

In this case, the steps in the chapter are the best way to answer that question:

1. **Step One:** Identify critical strategic account management performance needs within the context of the sales and customer management processes.
2. **Step Two:** Identify and speak to noncompetitive firms that have successfully implemented technology solutions for their strategic account management programs.
3. **Step Three:** Filter—which of these strategic account performance needs could technology best meet?
4. **Step Four:** Assess the technology-readiness of both the strategic account managers and anyone else who will be using the system.
5. **Step Five:** Develop and support tech-based solutions.
6. **Step Six:** Implementation—pilot, then rollout.
7. **Step Seven:** Review and revise tools..

From Analysis to Action . . . Ticonderoga Chemical and Strategic Account Management: The Payoff

Frank Piscatore, the VP of manufacturing at Goliath Corporation, felt himself besieged by executives from Hardin Chemical, one of his suppliers. He had received three calls for appointments that morning: from Hardin's VP of marketing, its director of sales, and its district manager. And he had received a similar call yesterday from its vice president/general manager. Each of the Hardin callers believed he had a compelling value offering for Piscatore and Goliath and all were vying for his time. And from the messages his secretary had taken for him, Piscatore saw that each of the Hardin executives was offering a significantly different value package. One offered an EDI system that Hardin had developed internally, one offered production-process consulting, and another offered a joint R&D project. Piscatore wondered whether Hardin's VPs were communicating with each other at all and he shook his head, wondering why they kept bothering him.

Piscatore left his office and headed for a meeting in which Bill Smith, the strategic account executive from Ticonderoga Chemical, another Goliath supplier, was officially kicking off the new EDI system that would link Ticonderoga and Goliath. Goliath had been piloting the new system over the last six months, and it had been earning all sorts of praise from Goliath decision makers. They were pleased with the abilities of the system but also with the way that Bill Smith had solicited their input and kept them up-to-date on the trial. Goliath's director of purchasing—one of Piscatore's direct reports—had been praising to the skies the EDI system's billing package, which offered electronic funds transfer, customized invoices, and virtually paperless purchasing. Ticonderoga's purchasing director, its IT staff, and Bill Smith had been working closely with Goliath's VP of purchasing on the system's functionality.

Piscatore had also heard glowing reports from his VP of sales, who suggested that they award Bill Smith and the Ticonderoga team their Supplier of the Year award. The VP of sales had been sold when Smith, over dinner, explained how the system would allow Goliath to check, order, and ship Ticonderoga inventory without having to call customer service representatives. At most of Goliath's suppliers, CSR's were either hard to reach or had to check with both inventory and shipping before they could call back with a realistic arrival date. This function would be a lifesaver to Goliath, allowing it to improve its own responsiveness to customers.

Piscatore had also heard from Goliath's VP of technology, who praised the functionality of the EDI system. The VP had spent many hours poring over the system's design specs with Smith, Ticonderoga's VP of MIS, and Ticonderoga programming people. The pilot had had some rocky moments but now the integration was virtually transparent.

Piscatore strolled into the meeting room to find Bill Smith chatting with Goliath's president. Normally the president would not have attended such a meeting, but Smith had copied him on all memos to Goliath executives regarding the new system's capabilities, its performance during the six-month trial, and, most important, the quantified cost savings that Goliath would realize from the system. Goliath's and Ticonderoga's financial people (including their respective CFOs) had worked with Bill Smith to show that the paperless billing system *alone* would save Goliath some $80,000 a year. That was the sort of news required to bring Goliath's normally reclusive president down to the meeting. Bill Smith stood up, thanking the Goliath executives for their aid with what he called "The Goliath System." He congratulated them on their ongoing and successful cost-cutting initiatives and, in a 15-minute slide presentation, he laid out the investments that both Goliath and Ticonderoga had made into the system's development and then the huge payback both firms would receive starting in six months. Given the system's value to Goliath, the decision was a no-brainer. Smith thanked Goliath for making Ticonderoga its sole-source chemical supplier, starting the next month.

Piscatore returned to his office, where he found three more messages from Hardin executives, all of whom wanted to schedule time with him. He tossed the messages into his wastebasket and sat back in his executive chair, calculating the impact of the new systems' savings on his profit-sharing check.

And far below Piscatore, in the bowels of Goliath, Don Brown, the Hardin key account seller, was trying to sell products to Goliath's technical people. He had no idea that Ticonderoga had just won a sole-source contract nor that they had been piloting an EDI system. He was not interested in understanding Goliath's business challenges, Goliath's needs, or how Goliath defined value. That would require too much time and Don needed to move more product to hit his quarterly sales target. Don was trying to sell Hardin products to anyone at Goliath whom he thought could buy.

So what had Bill Smith done to create the sole-source payoff? He had:

1. Developed a deep customer knowledge of Goliath Corporation, its business, and its organizational challenges.
2. Responded by offering a unique solution that would be a win for both Goliath and Ticonderoga.
3. Quantified the value of the EDI initiative to all executives.

4. Earned the trust of his customer to move to an exclusive relationship where the firms could act as partners.

Bill Smith had come from an organization that had done its homework, aligning on strategic accounts, developing support structures for SAMs , and standing ready to harvest those customers' opportunities.

CHAPTER 9

Conclusion: From Analysis to Action: Moving the Game Forward

In the conclusion, we'll discuss three topics:

1. The seven keys to managing strategic accounts.
2. The three benefits of strategic account management.
3. A game plan for moving forward.

Let's review: the seven keys to managing strategic accounts are:

Key 1: Define strategic account management as a business rather than a sales initiative. Unless everyone in the firm owns strategic accounts, value initiatives will take far too much time to design and implement. And even then the supplier may be one account phone call away from disaster.

Key 2: Create firm alignment and commitment to meet strategic accounts' needs and expectations. It's one thing to declare strategic account management a business initiative. It's a very different thing to get all supplier employees headed in roughly the same direction.

173

Key 3: Start with the right number of the right strategic accounts. Start with a few accounts that offer the greatest strategic opportunities.

Key 4: Create human resources support for strategic account management. Strategic accounts are probably your firm's greatest assets, but close behind them are your effective strategic account managers.

Key 5: Create firmwide relationships at multiple levels of relationships between the firm and its most critical accounts. Establish parallel linkages that raise emotional switching costs between you and your strategic accounts.

Key 6: Regularly quantify and communicate the value received from and delivered to strategic accounts. Remember: if you don't quantify value, it doesn't exist, either to your firm or to the accounts.

Key 7: Use technology judiciously. Technology solutions may seem dazzling but you need to approach them with high caution. Such solutions can create a prohibitive payback for strategic account management.

Are there other keys? Of course, and each firm will prioritize them and our keys differently. These are, however, the seven keys we believe any firm seeking successful strategic account management needs to deal with. If they do so thoughtfully and creatively, they can then reap the rewards of successful strategic account management (Figure 9–1).

F I G U R E 9–1

Benefits of Strategic Account Management

1. A sustainable competitive advantage.
2. Greater account loyalty.
3. Greater account profitability.

BENEFIT NUMBER ONE: STRATEGIC ACCOUNT MANAGEMENT'S SUSTAINABLE COMPETITIVE ADVANTAGE

Perhaps the greatest danger at an unaligned supplier is unmanaged customer interactions. When we, as customers, call such a firm for help and customer service cannot help us, too often we are shuffled around like vagrants, occasionally ending up in infinite voicemail loops. If we do speak to employees they may none-too-subtly communicate their lack of urgency to solve our problem, thus poisoning a golden marketing opportunity.

> At the heart of most business-to-business interactions are two people having a conversation.

Because that experience is all too common, a supplier can create a competitive advantage by aligning all of its functions on its most critical customers' expectations. This may sound like a business-to-customer approach, but at the heart of most business-to-business interactions are two people having a conversation.

When account contacts call aligned firms with questions or problems, there is no "that's not my job" response. Aligned employees know that maintaining customer loyalty is everyone's job. And such behavior does maintain—and increase—customer loyalty. When we call a firm where everyone tries to be helpful, our experience is so different, it creates a memorable impression. In aligned firms, customer service is not a department—it's an organizational commitment. And account contacts experience that commitment in virtually every call.

> In aligned firms customer service is not a department—it's an organizational commitment.

Aligning a firm around strategic accounts starts with a firm aligning itself after systematically learning accounts' expectations. The firm then shares those expectations with all employees and asks them what the company needs to do to meet and exceed those customers' expectations consistently. The firm transforms employee answers into systems and processes for the company to develop and implement. Even though we say this in three sentences, firm alignment takes at least 12 to 36 months because it requires substantial organizational commitment, communication, and self-discipline. As with most of life's challenges, it's far easier to state our resolve than to actually develop and focus it long term.

> **As with most of life's challenges, it's far easier to state our resolve than to actually develop and focus it long term.**

Once established, though, firm alignment tends to create a virtuous cycle, in which employees work smarter, not harder, and where teamwork increases employee satisfaction, customer satisfaction, firm productivity, and profitability. This cycle, once started, makes it doubly difficult for competitors to duplicate service and relationship quality levels. Get most employees headed in the same direction and few things can stop them—unless customers change their expectations or employees get shifted to other priorities. To prevent priority shifting, we return to how critical it is to get the long-term buy-in of all firm executives. If any of them acts as if this commitment is flexible, they can turn alignment into another program *du jour*.

> **[W]hen sustainable competitive advantages are harder and harder to come by, aligning a firm around its strategic accounts offers just such an advantage.**

This can instill or reinforce employee cynicism and can sometimes create higher cross-functional barriers for customers to leap over. "That's not my job" can return with a vengeance.

If a firm can stay the course, though, the competitive advantage can become sustainable—*if* the firm continues to monitor customer expectations and redirect itself when those expectations change. The good news here is that, once employees align and focus on customer expectations, experiencing the firm as team, it becomes that much easier to redirect their efforts to serve changing customer needs. This is not the case with unaligned competitors, who still have to climb the first—and highest—mountain. At a time when sustainable competitive advantages are harder and harder to come by, aligning a firm around its strategic accounts offers just such an advantage.

BENEFIT NUMBER TWO: STRATEGIC ACCOUNT MANAGEMENT'S GREATER ACCOUNT LOYALTY

Strategic account management can create greater customer loyalty, which in turn can create greater customer profitability. There has been a great deal of research into what customer loyalty can mean for a supplier. In *The Loyalty Effect,* Fred Reichheld makes a compelling case that a 5 percent increase in retention leads to a 35 percent to 95 percent increase in the customer's net present value.[1] While Reichheld bases his figures on retail relationships, the principle holds true in business-to-business relationships. Given the value of most strategic accounts, these loyalty numbers can become very dramatic over time. David Jones, a management consultant, provided us with both business-to-business and business-to-consumer examples:

> One of the world's largest telecommunications firms has clearly seen the benefits of establishing relationships with its strategic accounts. After it made the shift from a transactional to a relationship-based approach, its annual customer churn rates fell dramatically. For customers buying more than three products, customer retention was 99 percent compared with about 40 percent several years before.

---

[1]   Reichheld, Frederick F. (1996). *The Loyalty Effect: The Hidden Force Behind Growth, Profits, and Lasting Value* (p.36). Boston: Harvard University Press.

The value of relationships can also be seen in mass markets in the telecommunications industry. BellSouth's Complete Choice plan, for example, provides customers with an array of services such as call block, call waiting, caller ID, etc. for one monthly price. It also serves as an excellent base from which to sell cellular service, long distance, and other services. The Company has found that customers who buy even one additional service have "dramatically higher" than average retention rates."[2]

How can strategic account management drive greater loyalty and profitability? For the most complex relationships, where decentralized suppliers are serving decentralized customers, the number of possible errors rises geometrically, as do the number of actual errors. A strategic account manager, acting as the single point of ownership and given the right level of power to make decisions, can help solve these issues as they arise. At the same time, the account manager can think longer-term and start to set up systems and processes to limit recurring problems and make selling and buying a much easier proposition for both sides. Ease of doing business is an almost universal expectation of strategic accounts.

If the SAM has the firm aligned behind her, she will almost certainly be orchestrating relationships between her firm and the strategic account. Each of these function-to-function and executive-to-executive relationships (as well as being a compelling value equation) creates another tether between the two firms until, ideally, the bonds are exceedingly hard to break. We've already seen what can happen when there are few interfirm relationships: one transfer, one new buyer influence, one promotion, and the entire dynamics of the relationship can change—if not disappear. To increase loyalty and long-term customer value, the strategic account manager needs to ask himself continually how he can deepen and broaden the relationship with the account. Generally speaking, the more working relationships, the more layers of loyalty. The greater the loyalty, the greater can be the customer's value over time.

---

[2]   David Jones, in an email to the authors, November 11, 2002.

BENEFIT NUMBER THREE: STRATEGIC ACCOUNT MANAGEMENT'S GREATER ACCOUNT PROFITABILITY

Alignment around strategic accounts offers another potential benefit: higher-profit sales. Forming relationships, treating those relationships as assets, and investing in maintaining those assets can jack up retention and thus the relationships' value. At the same time, SAMs can shift from selling products to selling firm competencies and increased account productivity. The profit for such sales tends to be higher because the account is willing to pay more for the greater value the supplier offers. It is one thing to sell an account a warehouse; it's another thing altogether to take over the account's entire warehousing operations. The same thing holds true for joint research and development or joint marketing projects that can create new technologies or new markets for both firms. Opportunities in strategic account relationships abound for the strategic account manager with deep customer knowledge.

Attempting to sell strategically to a transactional account is similar to burning a thousand-dollar bill for heat.

Granted, there are large accounts that use their volume to force price breaks and greater service levels, both of which can torpedo supplier margins. That situation takes us back to the critical selection of the right accounts, particularly strategic rather than transactional buyers. Attempting to sell strategically to a transactional account is similar to burning a thousand-dollar bill for heat.

If large accounts in your industry tend to be transactionally oriented, you might strategically focus on other relationships—high-opportunity, medium-sized accounts, for example. Again: strategic accounts most easily allow you to achieve your strategic and financial goals. There is no size requirement. When you commit to an account relationship that buys strategically, though, your approach turns from selling product to selling more profitable business solutions.

As an example of how selling productivity rather than products can create higher-profit sales, consider the Marriott-Deloitte & Touche story.

THE MARRIOTT-DELOITTE & TOUCHE STORY

Imagine you're a global firm and one day, a major division shows up and finds all its buildings condemned. You have 600 employees and thousands of clients, some major firms themselves, depending on you. The situation is not hypothetical. The lower Manhattan practice of Deloitte & Touche (D&T), a global professional services firm, showed up at World Financial Center on September 12, 2001 to find that the collapse of the World Trade Center had severely damaged the D&T office building. The employees had no access to their offices, their computers, and their phones. Tax season, their busiest time, was looming.

D&T sent out an RFP for temporary office space to several major hotel chains, among them Marriott International. Their RFP seemed pretty straightforward. D&T was looking for 200–250 offices for a minimum of two months—starting immediately. As Patrice Spinner, the Marriott International Alliance Account Sales Director for D&T said, a typical hotel response would have been to offer availability and pricing. And most chains responded to D&T that way.

But Spinner wanted to play a different game. She and other Marriott managers formed a cross-functional account management team that created a total solution for D&T. The team included managers from Marriott's Global Sales Organization, a hotel general manager, Marriott sales executives, a regional general manager from Marriott's ExecuStay's furniture rental division, a regional VP of information resources and her six-person team (who themselves assembled a team of a half dozen IR, systems managers, and data service engineers to orchestrate setting up phone, computer, and Internet lines), the general manager of Marriott's Worldwide Reservation Center, and many others.

The Marriott team's solution included room pricing and availability, plus safety and security systems, food and beverage options, telecommunications (Internet connections, phone banks, etc.), office furniture rental (Marriott was the only firm with a furniture rental division—about which Spinner knew nothing before this project), consolidated billing, and customer service. The team goal, included in the Marriott proposal, was to "deliver a comprehensive office relocation package that provides Deloitte & Touche with virtually uninterrupted service to clients." This is a value proposition far beyond rooms.

Marriott won the bid. Then began the implementation, whose logistics were staggering. Hundred of D&T employees needed office space as well as the communications infrastructure required by a high-tech business. At the same time, all D&T clients needed immediate access to their associates. When D&T awarded the contract, overnight it moved computers, files, staff, etc., from its financial center offices to a Marriott hotel.

Normally the time frame on a job this large would have been weeks or even months. But working together, the Marriott team (Spinner's "volunteer army") readied the hotel for occupancy in 12 days. Spinner had met the team's goal of creating a solution so total that all D&T needed to do was check in. And check in they did on September 24—just four days after the contract was signed.

The glue that held D&T and the clients together was Marriott's turnkey customer service package. Marriott even set up and staffed a call center to take D&T's incoming calls. Marriott had its people trained in how to take calls for D&T, and they now handle approximately 800 to 1,000 calls daily, routing each to the correct office or voice mail. To D&T clients, the service was transparent.

THE VALUE DELIVERED TO DELOITTE & TOUCHE

The value Deloitte & Touche reaped is difficult to determine with precision, but Marriott, in effect, allowed the New York City-based D&T tax practice to continue to do business. Six hundred D&T associates, who otherwise would have lacked both office and support, now had a home in NYC where they could immediately achieve high productivity. In these offices, they could also be with fellow associates, many of whom had personally experienced the tragedy of September 11th. How many billable hours can 600 associates generate in a month? In two months? Three?

THE VALUE DELIVERED TO MARRIOTT INTERNATIONAL

The value Marriott received? The contract totaled 230 rooms per night, seven days a week. The Marriott hotel, which had been a leader in occupancy not only within Marriott but in NYC, suddenly found itself experiencing terribly low occupancy after September 11th and had been unsure what the next few months would bring. The contract has thus far generated $14+ million in incremental revenue for Marriott, with the near certainty that D&T will exercise its option to continue this arrangement. This incremental revenue was more than the rooms alone would have cost D&T—but so was the value D&T received.

This is a clear case of delivering significant value to the account and the supplier. The Marriott cross-functional team, without which Spinner admits she would not have been able to win the business, received nothing from having been a part of the team—except the satisfaction of having done a spectacular job for a major client. Spinner described her role as the team "coach," overseeing the project management. The total solution has worked so well that, whenever a problem does arise, it is quickly solved. The Marriott and Deloitte & Touche relationship continues to deepen as the two firms find it increasingly easy to work together.

There are other ways in which strategic account relationships reap higher profits. As loyalty increases, revenue flow becomes more predictable, acquisition costs go down, and firms get used to doing business with each other. While it is difficult to quantify the value of a more familiar firm interface, most firms recognize which suppliers are easy to do business with and which are not.

A sustainable competitive advantage, greater account loyalty, and higher-profit sales—these are benefits most suppliers would move heaven and earth for. But while describing these advantages, we have skimmed over some of the less quantifiable but nonetheless real benefits—increased employee satisfaction because of the new team-based organization, greater efficiencies through lowered functional barriers, and a greater employee ability to change focus—*if* the change request comes from the account. These three items can drive a firm's continuing success in the marketplace.

A GAME PLAN FOR MOVING FORWARD

Now let's look at a high-level implementation plan to achieve these benefits, drawing on our seven keys. This is not meant to be a definitive implementation map, which couldn't exist anyway. As Tom VanHootegem of Boise Office Solutions told us in a January 2003 phone call, "There is no 'plug-and-play' strategic account implementation plan."

Firms will need to arrive at strategic account management in their own way. The graphic does deal, though, with the critical issues we feel firms need to face (see Figure 9–2).

The chart starts with the eight elements of a strategic account management program, all but one of which (products and services) we have covered in this book. With those elements in mind, you can examine and/or take the getting-started actions.

THE GETTING-STARTED ACTIONS

We have discussed customer assessments and how critical it is to capture customers' expectations and concerns before developing a strategic account management program. If you find two large customers who are solely interested in lower price, for example, you can save yourself a great deal of investment. But here also is a rare opportunity for leveraging research: use video focus groups as a part of these assessments, and you will have a way of demonstrating what the customer said to all

Planning and Implementing a Strategic Account Management Program (SAMP)

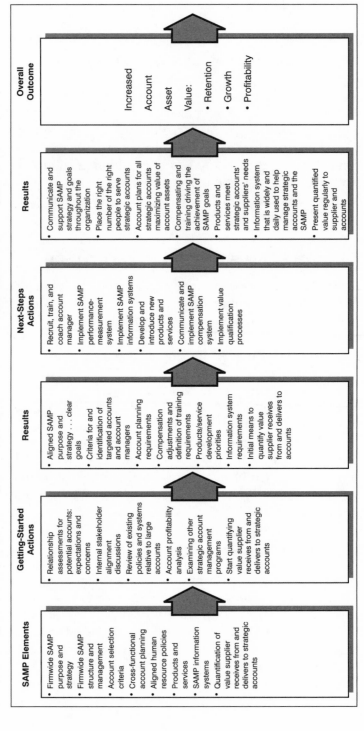

those employees supporting strategic account management. Video focus groups, where the customers directly address the viewer, are a powerful way to help create alignment. And, at the beginning of such a tape, when the customers introduce themselves, we strongly suggest using a graphic overlay showing the 10-year value of the customer's business. The overlay changes a talking head into a multimillion-dollar voice. That way it becomes much easier for everyone to see how much that customer's good opinion means to the firm.

Once the company gathers the customer data, it's time to start having the cross-functional alignment discussions that will ensure that the strategic account management program will be a business rather than a pure sales initiative. The approach has to generate short- and long-term sales, yes, but as a business initiative, the program will generate more revenue if the entire supplier is actively behind it. Strategic account managers will have to spend significantly less time selling projects internally if the firm is already on board.

These alignment discussions involve looking at the ways in which the supplier currently deals with strategic accounts. Supplier policies, practices, and systems can deal with such customers. It will be very important to study them and to determine from the accounts which of them is working and which is not. For example, how many personal relationships—both inside the supplier and at the customers—do SAMs currently have to manage?

It's also time to do a portfolio analysis on potential strategic accounts—as in-depth a view of customer profitability as possible. In some cases, this analysis can teach you more than you want to know about your large customers. Given the investment a strategic account management program takes, it's better to identify true returns before designating a given customer as a strategic account. Basing potential returns solely on revenue or averaged profits can cost a firm a great deal.

A supplier can also examine other successful strategic account management approaches. This used to be far more challenging, but now, with new sources and conferences available (including those put on by the Strategic Account Management

Association), you can hear presentations from and maybe even get an introduction to directors of successful strategic account management programs. Usually a noncompetitive firm is willing to answer questions; occasionally it will let you come speak to a contact there.

Value quantification is crucial to strategic account management success. A group of executives can start to develop a profitability model for targeted customers as well as a model to quantify the value of delivered products and services. Recall the words of the strategic account manager in Chapter 6: "Unless it is quantified, value doesn't exist."

The results of the getting-started actions include, most importantly, an aligned strategic account management program (SAMP) purpose and strategy—commitment from various functions to support the efforts of the SAMP. This includes agreements and processes by which multiple functions can effectively work together.

With customer input about the level of account manager contact desired, the supplier can work backward to determine an appropriate staffing model. The one presented in Chapter 5 is an effective way to cross-validate how many relationships an account manager should manage.

RESULTS

The items in the "Results" column are critical support issues, such as having developed account and account manager selection criteria, account planning requirements, appropriate compensation and training plans, specifications for a strategic account management information system, and an initial way to quantify the value you receive from and deliver to strategic accounts.

The next two columns in the graphic provide another iteration of steps and results, all of which lead to increased customer retention, growth, and profitability. As we have said, this roadmap is not intended to be a definitive implementation plan. It does, however, deal with issues that, if the supplier does not face them, can quickly turn into the costly implementation errors presented throughout this book.

We know a consultant who says that, in the next 10 years, selling will evolve into either strategic account management or Internet auctions, with few offerings in between. We think that statement goes too far. But many firms in many markets have started to differentiate themselves through their strategic account management programs. This differentiation puts competitors in a bind: they either move to some form of strategic account management or they are forced to compete on price. If they do the former, the firm they are following has a huge first-mover advantage, with alignment and delivery processes up and running. If they choose to compete on price, they create a downward margin spiral.

To summarize, strategic account management:

1. Creates a sustainable competitive advantage.
2. Creates greater account loyalty.
3. Provides greater account profitability.

Strategic account management does these things by being more relationship-oriented and more flexible and innovative than the competition, by providing quantified value, and by meeting and raising its customers' expectations. Assuming its buying orientation is strategic, a customer will respond to strategic account management—sometimes so strongly that the supplier feels almost immediately justified in investing more resources in the account management program. The more value the supplier provides, the more value the account can provide. The relationship thus becomes a highly profitable closed loop, with competitors, forced out of the equation, knocking at the customers' doors but not necessarily getting in (as we saw with Hardin Chemical in the story that introduced this part). We have seen this happen locally, regionally, nationally, and globally.

If you are thinking about moving to strategic account management or refining your current program, consider what you want to accomplish, determine the executive help you are going to need, and then start moving forward. This book provides what we believe are the keys—and inversely the pitfalls—to implementing a strategic account management program, as well as describes firms that have overcome those pitfalls.

You are now armed with a mission and an initial high-level implementation plan. You are poised to start the challenging and rewarding job of aligning your firm with accounts' expectations. Move systematically, thoughtfully, include all stakeholders and, while success is never guaranteed, you will at least have a greater opportunity to do it right the first time. Good luck and good results.

REFERENCES

Hamel, G. and C. K. Prahalad (1994). *Competing for the Future: Breakthrough Strategies for Seizing Control of Your Industry and Creating the Markets of Tomorrow* (p. 4). Boston: Harvard Business School Press.

Heiman, S. E. and D. Sanchez (1998). *The New Strategic Selling: The Unique Sales System Proven Successful by the World's Best Companies* (pp. 68-69). New York: Warner Books.

Maister, David H., et al (2000). *The Trusted Advisor*. New York: The Free Press.

Miller, R. B. and S. E. Heiman (1992). *Successful Large Account Management*. New York: Warner Books.

Rackham, N., L. Friedman, and R. Ruff (1996). *Getting Partnering Right: How Market Leaders Are Creating Long-Term Competitive Advantage* (p. 59). New York, McGraw-Hill.

Reichheld, F. (1996). *The Loyalty Effect: The Hidden Force Behind Growth, Profits, and Lasting Value* (p. 36). Boston: Harvard Business School Press.

Senge, P. M. (1990). *The Fifth Discipline: The Art and Practice of the Learning Organization* (p. 234). New York: Currency.

Stauffer, David (2002). "Five Missteps to Avoid in Volatile Times" (p. 3). *Harvard Management Update,* September, Volume 7, Number 9.

INDEX